CIVIL LITIGATION, EVIDENCE AND REMEDIES

2014 – 2015

Daniel Khoo

Thomas Windsor

ISBN: 1500975168
ISBN-13: 978-1500975166

Dedicated to our families,

with thanks for their unending support.

FOREWORD

This 'little blue book' has been a dream of mine since I first grappled with the civil litigation exam on the BVC. In those days there were only MCQ's to contend with and only an imperfect manual to help. Fast forward to the Wood Review and the BSB's introduction of centrally set assessments and it is no longer possible to learn the rules 'parrot fashion' or to aggregate scores on the civil paper. BPTC students must demonstrate a thorough understanding of civil litigation and apply it accurately in challenging short answer questions. Whilst the White Book holds all the answers, it can seem impenetrable at times and a simplified guide, designed specifically for those sitting civil litigation, is therefore long overdue.

If I had been asked to handpick the authors of such a book, I would have chosen Daniel Khoo and Tom Windsor. They epitomise all that I hope for in a BPTC student: they are personable, diligent and supremely intelligent. Their respective résumés belie the fact that they graduated in the top 5% of the highest achieving BPTC cohort since the inception of the centrally set papers. They have produced a book that is comprehensive, accurate and outstanding. I am delighted they accepted the gauntlet and I recommend that every budding lawyer buys a copy of this 'little blue book' which I predict will become an essential codicil to the White Book.

Lynda Gibbs
BPTC Design Director, University of Law

INTRODUCTION

Civil Litigation, Evidence and Remedies is the most challenging examination on the Bar Professional Training Course. The course requires a strong grasp of difficult concepts and particular attention to detail. Over the last three years failure rates have remained significantly increased. In 2013 and 2014 over 40% of students failed the exam on the first sitting.

This book is intended as an overview and revision guide. It is based upon and closely follows the structure of the 2014 – 2015 syllabus for Civil Litigation, Evidence and Remedies.[1] It contains numerous tables and diagrams aimed at simplifying the key rules. The result is that the reader has the foundations for each section of the syllabus in concisely structured chapters.

On 1 June 2013, the majority of recommendations by Sir Rupert Jackson in his Review of Civil Litigation Costs (2009)[2] were implemented. Parts 43 – 48 of the Civil Procedure Rules 'CPR' have received a radical overhaul as a result. This has had a knock-on effect throughout the rest of the CPR. Civil legal aid has simultaneously been transformed through the Legal Aid, Sentencing and Punishment of Offenders Act 2012 'LASPO'.

A GUIDE TO USING THIS BOOK

This book is aimed at students on the BPTC course and assumes that the reader has a law degree or the Graduate Diploma in Law.

Points of importance in the body of text are in **bold**. References to statutes and procedural rules are underlined, for example: CPR 1.1. It is highly recommended that each underlined reference to the CPR is read simultaneous in the White Book. Each chapter ends with a Chapter Summary that highlights important rules.

---

[1] To the extent that readers will note that Chapter 19, as in the syllabus, is simply 'not used'

[2] Referred to throughout as 'the Jackson reforms'

ABOUT THE AUTHORS

Daniel Khoo BA (Oxon), BCL

Daniel has a BA in Jurisprudence with French Law from Oxford University. In 2013 he obtained a Distinction on the Bachelor of Civil Law and was awarded the Clifford Chance prize for the best performance in Principles of Civil Procedure. He was awarded Outstanding on the BPTC and Outstanding in the Civil Litigation, Evidence and Remedies exam.

Thomas Windsor LLB (Exon), BCL, Barrister

Thomas graduated at the top of his year with an LLB in Law from Exeter University. He obtained a Distinction on the Bachelor of Civil Law at Oxford University in 2013. In 2014, he was awarded Outstanding on the BPTC and received the Best Advocate prize.

COMMON ABBREVIATIONS

Common abbreviations used throughout the text are:

A	Applicant
ATE	After The Event (insurance)
AoS	Acknowledgement of Service
BTE	Before The Event (insurance)
C	Claimant
CA	Court of Appeal
CC	Counterclaim
CFA	Conditional Fee Arrangement
ChD	Chancery Division of the High Court
CMC	Case Management Conference
CN	Contributory Negligence
CPR	Civil Procedure Rules
D	Defendant
D2	Second Defendant
DBA	Damages Based Agreement
DJ	District Judge
HCJ	High Court judge
JC	Judgment Creditor

JD	Judgment Debtor
JR	Judicial Review
LAA	Legal Aid Agency
LPP	Legal Professional Privilege
PD	Practice Direction
PI	Personal Injury
PII	Public Interest Immunity
QBD	Queen's Bench Division of the High Court
QOCS	Qualified One-Way Costs Shifting
R	Respondent
RX	Re-examination
RTA	Road Traffic Accident
SC	Supreme Court
TP	Third Party
W	Witness
W/S	Witness Statement
XIC	Examination in Chief
XX	Cross Examination

We are very grateful to Anthony Kennedy who reviewed the manuscript and Lynda Gibbs without whom the book would not have been written. It should go without saying that all errors remain our own.

Every effort has been made to state the law as applicable on 1 September 2014.

TABLE OF CONTENTS

1. ORGANISATIONAL OUTLINE

This chapter gives a brief overview of the organisation of the courts. Closely related chapters are Chapter 4 (Commencing Proceedings), Chapter 14 (Case Management) and Chapter 26 (Appeals).

1.1. Organisation of the High Court (outline)

The High Court is divided into three divisions. Within each division there are specialist courts for certain types of proceedings:

Divisions of the High Court		
Queen's Bench Division	Family Division	Chancery Division
Commercial Court	Court of Protection	Patents Court
Technology and Construction Court[3]		
Admiralty Court		
Mercantile Court		Company Court
Administrative Court		

The High Court is normally constituted by a single High Court Judge ('HCJ'). Procedural matters may be dealt with by a Master.

1.2. Organisation of the county court (outline)

The county court sits in 92 towns and cities. It is presided over by a DJ or a Circuit Judge.

---

[3] The Technology and Construction Court can also sit in the ChD

1.3. Allocation of business between the High and county court (outline)

Most of the rules allocating cases between the High and county court are contained in PD 7A.

Some claims can only be started in the High Court. They are:
➢ Judicial Review
➢ Contentious probate where the value of the land is greater than £30,000
➢ Libel, slander, toll, market or franchise claims (unless the parties agree in writing)
➢ Claim for damages for a judicial act under the Human Rights Act 1998

Some claims can only be started in the county court. They are:
➢ Claims in respect of regulated consumer credit agreements[4]
➢ Most possession, landlord and tenant claims[5]
➢ PI claims worth less than or equal to £50,000
➢ Non-PI claims less than or equal to £100,000

Where both the High Court and county court have jurisdiction over the claim the claim may be started in either court. The factors that determine the more appropriate court are:
➢ The financial value of the claim
➢ The complexity of facts, legal issues, remedies or procedures
➢ Any public importance

---

[4] PD 7B [4.1]
[5] CPR 55 and CPR 56

1.4. Allocation of business between tracks

The High Court and the county court will allocate every claim to one of three tracks based on the following:

Small claims track	Fast track	Multi-track
Claims for < £10k	£10k < claim < £25k	Claims > £25k
PI claims where <1k of PSLA claimed	Claims where the trial will last < 1 day	All Part 8 claims (see Chapter 4)
Housing disrepair claims where: ➢ Repairs < £1k, and ➢ Damages < £1k	Claims where expert evidence will not exceed: ➢ Two expert fields ➢ One expert per field per party	
	Claims for less than £10k involving a disputed allegation of dishonesty	

Directions questionnaire[6]
The court provisionally allocates the case after D files their Defence. The court will serve a notice of proposed allocation on the parties. The parties then complete a directions questionnaire. The time limits are:
- ➢ Small claims: 14 days after service of notice of proposed allocation
- ➢ Fast / Multi-track: 28 days after service of notice of proposed allocation

The court will then allocate the case. It may hold a hearing if the parties do not agree about where to allocate the case.

---

[6] CPR 26.3

Sanction for failing to complete directions questionnaire[7]
There is a difference between designated and non-designated money claims (see Chapter 4.1).

In a designated money claim, the court will:
- ➢ Give the party in breach 7 further days, then
- ➢ Strike out the claim

In a non-designated money claim the court will make an order as appropriate (e.g. strike out, or ordering a hearing to determine allocation).

1.5. Overriding objective of the CPR

The overriding objective of the CPR is designed to guide the courts in their application of all the procedural rules and discretion.

CPR 1.1 states:
> (1) These Rules are a new procedural code with the overriding objective of enabling the court to deal with cases justly and at proportionate cost.
> ...

CPR 1.1(2) goes on to expand a number of considerations required by the overriding objective. It includes a **new post-Jackson consideration** that the court should enforce compliance with rules, PDs and orders.

1.6. Impact of the Human Rights Act 1998 on civil claims

Section 3 of the Human Rights Act 1998 requires the courts to read primary and secondary legislation in such a way as to be compatible with the European Convention on Human Rights.

Section 6 of the Human Rights Act 1998 requires the courts, as public authorities, to act in a manner compatible with the European Convention on Human Rights.

---

[7] CPR 26.3 (7A) and (8)

Both sections mean that the Convention rights can have an impact on civil claims.

CHAPTER SUMMARY

➤ The specialist courts in the HC have their own practice guides found in Volume II of the White Book.

➤ Courts are no longer merely concerned in dealing with cases justly. Following the Jackson reforms, emphasis is also placed on proportionate cost.

➤ The list of considerations in <u>CPR 1.1(2)</u> is a useful guide to the application of <u>CPR 1.1.</u>

2. PRE-ACTION PROTOCOLS

The courts expect the parties to a case to clarify the main issues in dispute by cooperating during pre-action investigations. The hope is that more informed parties are better placed to assess the merits of their case and as a result may choose to make early offers to settle.

2.1. The Practice Direction (Pre-Action Conduct)

PD: Pre-Action Conduct covers the following:
> The approach of the courts
> The principles governing the conduct of the parties in cases not subject to a pre-action protocol
> Requirements that apply in all cases

General principles of pre-action conduct:
> Exchanging sufficient information to enable comprehension of the other side's case
> Making appropriate attempts to resolve the dispute without resorting to bringing proceedings (including considering ADR)

2.2. List of specific pre-action protocols

Certain types of case have a specific pre-action protocol:
> Personal Injury
> Low Value RTAs
> Clinical Negligence
> Disease and Illness
> Rent arrears
> Housing Disrepair
> Mortgage possession
> Commercial property dilapidations
> Construction and engineering
> Professional negligence
> Defamation
> Judicial review

2.3. Principles relating to pre-action conduct under the PI Pre-Action Protocol

The <u>Pre-Action Protocol: PI</u> is primarily designed for PI claims **worth up to £25,000**. However, the **spirit** of the protocol should still be followed in higher value cases.

Low value (£1,000 to £10,000) RTA claims are covered by the specific <u>Pre-Action Protocol: Low Value RTA</u>.

The parties can depart from the detail of the PI Protocol but the court will want an explanation of the reasons for doing so once proceedings are subsequently issued.

General timeline of pre-action conduct:

Step	Comment
C sends informal letter to D or D's insurer	Not strictly required by the Protocol but good practice
C sends D a letter before claim	The start of the formal protocol procedure. D has 21 days to acknowledge, naming an insurer
D sends an acknowledgement	D's acknowledgment within 21 days naming an insurer
D investigates	D or D's insurer then has 3 months in which to investigate the allegations
D disputes: denial letter	If D disputes the allegations, then D replies with a denial letter and discloses all documents relevant to liability
Contributory negligence	If contributory negligence is alleged by D, C should respond within a reasonable time
Medical evidence from C	Medical evidence must be obtained based on C's injuries
Negotiation or ADR considered	Before starting proceedings, C and D are encouraged to negotiate or enter into ADR procedures

2.4. The details of pre-action conduct where no specific protocol applies: Section III PD: Pre-Action Conduct and Annex A PD: Pre-Action Conduct

In cases not covered by a published protocol, parties must comply with the **ethos** of the guidance given in the Practice Direction: Pre-Action Conduct.

The published protocols do **not** cover most commercial and contractual claims, or many other types of litigation.

In cases not covered by an approved protocol, the parties should act in accordance with the overriding objective. This means reasonably exchanging information and documents relevant to the claim and trying to avoid court proceedings.

General timeline for pre-action conduct:

Step	Comment
C sends D a letter before claim	C writes a detailed letter before claim setting out the facts and basis of the claim, as well as the documents C relies on
CFA or ATE notification	If either C or D has entered into a CFA or taken out ATE insurance, they must notify the other side immediately
D has a reasonable time to reply	The reasonable time to reply is based on the nature of the case (ranging from 14 days for a simple debt to 90 days for more complex matters)
D replies	D's response to the detailed letter before claim should indicate whether liability is accepted in full, in part or is denied
Preliminary exchange of documents	Both C and D may ask the other for copies of relevant documents possessed by the other side (note: their use is limited to the purpose of resolution of this dispute)
Negotiation or ADR considered	Both C and D should consider negotiation and other forms of ADR: both parties should retain evidence of having at least considered this

2.5. Non-compliance with pre-action protocols: PD: Pre-action Conduct [4.6]

Non-compliance with the pre-action protocols may be justified in some circumstances. For example, if the limitation period is about to expire, a party may be justified in issuing to prevent being time-barred. In such a case there may be no sanction. By contrast, deliberate failures may result in court sanctions at a later stage.

If, taking into account the overall effect of any non-compliance, the court decides to impose a sanction, it may:

➤ Order a stay of proceedings to allow compliance
➤ Make a costs order against the party at fault

- ➤ Order the party at fault to pay those costs on an indemnity basis
- ➤ If the party at fault is C who eventually succeeds, deprive that party of interest (or award interest at a lower rate), or
- ➤ If the party at fault is D who eventually loses, award interest at a higher rate.

The court may also make an order that the defaulting party should pay a sum of money into court if the default was without good reason.[8]

CHAPTER SUMMARY

- ➤ PD: Pre-Action Conduct provides guidance as to expected pre-action conduct where the 12 protocols do not apply.
- ➤ The courts increasingly impose sanctions if parties fail to comply with the protocols or PD.

---

[8] CPR 3.1(5)

3. LIMITATION

Limitation of civil actions restrict the time in which parties can sue. Most of English law has been codified in the Limitation Act 1980 ('LA'). Limitation provides individuals and businesses with a degree of certainty.

3.1. Calculating limitation

Accrual

In order to work out whether a limitation period has expired it is important to know the event that triggers the start of the period (when 'time begins to run'). Limitation starts on the 'accrual' of the cause of action, which is the point at which the cause of action becomes complete.

Accrual therefore gives rise to an important difference between contract and many torts. As under English law **any** breach of contract is actionable (i.e. can be sued upon) the cause of action for breach of contract accrues on breach (not damage) and so time runs from the date of breach.

By contrast, in many torts, including the tort of negligence, damage is a requirement for the tort. Time only begins to run from the time of damage for the tort of negligence. However, caution is needed: some torts are actionable without proof of damage.

When time stops

Time stops running for the purpose of limitation when a Claim Form is received at the court for issue (not when the Claim Form is served). If the court is closed on the last day of limitation, if the Claim Form is received the next working day, it will be in time.[9]

---

[9] *Kaur v Russell* [1973] QB 337

19

Relation back

Defences of set-off or counterclaim are deemed to have been issued on the day that a claim was issued. Therefore a counterclaim that would otherwise have been out of time can be made, so long as the claim to which it relates was made in time.

3.2. Simple limitation periods

In all cases time runs from accrual:

Type of action	Limitation period	Statutory reference
Tort	6 years	s 2 LA
Contract	6 years	s 5 LA
Recovery of land	12 years	s 15 LA
Contribution claims	2 years	s 10 LA
Judicial review	3 months	(see Chapter 25.2)

3.3. Limitation in PI and fatal accident cases

Limitation period

The limitation period is 3 years. It runs from the later of:
- ➢ Date of injury / death, or
- ➢ Date of knowledge

Knowledge: s 14 LA

The knowledge C needs for limitation to start is that:
- ➢ The injury is sufficiently serious to justify commencing,
- ➢ The injury is attributable to D's breach of duty,
- ➢ The identity of D, and
- ➢ (where act / omission was not of D but TP), the identity of that TP [e.g. for vicarious liability]

The knowledge C has includes knowledge that C might be reasonably expected to acquire. It may be reasonable to expect C to consult an expert or lawyer.

3.4. Discretion to extend time in PI and fatal accident cases

The court has a broad discretion to extend the 3 years in a PI or fatal accident case by virtue of s 33 LA. The court must have regard to:
> The balance of prejudice suffered by C and D by the delay
> The length of the delay
> The reasons for the delay
> D's conduct, and
> The extent that evidence is likely to be less cogent

Where the failure is partially due to a lawyer, C may have the option of suing the lawyer for loss of the chance to sue.

3.5. Latent damage and limitation

There are special rules extending limitation for latent (hidden) damage. They only apply to non-PI and non-fatal accident **negligence** claims.

By s 14A LA limitation in negligence is the later of:
> 6 years from the date of accrual (the normal period), or
> 3 years from the date of knowledge

Knowledge is defined as for PI cases above.

Section 15B LA provides for a 15 year 'longstop' on latent damage negligence claims. It runs from the date of the act or omission that is alleged to be negligent.

3.6. Disabilities and limitation

Disability does not mean physical disability. It refers to:
> Children (disabled until they reach 18 years of age), or
> Protected parties (disabled while protected)

Time does not begin to run until the party is no longer under a disability: s 28 LA.

3.7. Fraud, concealment and mistake: s 32 LA

Action based upon fraud

Time does not run until C discovers, or could reasonably have discovered the fraud.

Fact relevant to cause of action deliberately concealed

Time does not run until C discovers, or could reasonably have discovered the concealment.

Following *Williams v Fanshaw*[10] the fact concealed must be one that:
- ➤ D had a duty to disclose, or
- ➤ D would have disclosed in the normal course of the relationship, but D decided not to disclose

Action for mistake

Time does not run until C discovers, or could reasonably have discovered the mistake. Mistake must be an essential element of the cause of action (e.g. money paid in consequence of a mistake). The mistake can be one of law or fact.

CHAPTER SUMMARY

- ➤ Limitation begins to run at different times for different claims.
- ➤ Limitation does not run against children under 18 years.
- ➤ There are special rules relating to hidden damage in negligence claims.
- ➤ The court can extend time in a PI claim.

---

[10] [2004] EWCA Civ 157

4. Commencing Proceedings

This chapter deals with how C starts a claim against D. C issues a claim with the court, either under Part 7 or Part 8. The claim is then served on D. For D's response to C's claim, see Chapter 6.5.

4.1. Part 7 claims

Part 7 is named after and governed by CPR 7 and its Practice Directions. They are the 'normal' type of claim.

Scope

A Part 7 claim should be used where:
  ➢ There is likely to be a substantial dispute of fact, and
  ➢ No rule or PD requires Part 8

Content

For the content of a Part 7 claim, see Chapter 6.3.

Formalities

Part 7 claims must:
  ➢ Contain a statement of truth, and
  ➢ Include a form for defending or admitting the claim and Acknowledgement of Service

Part 7 claims may contain the Particulars of Claim. If they do not, the Particulars of Claim must be served within 14 days of service of the Claim Form.

Venue

Claims for a specified or unspecified sum in the county court are designated money claims and should be commenced in the Court Money Claims Centre in Salford. The claim will be issued out of Northampton County Court and then transferred if D files a Defence (see further Chapter 14 on Case Management).

4.2. Part 8 claims

Scope

A Part 8 claim should be used where:
- ➢ There is no substantial dispute of fact, for example:
  - ○ Approval of a settlement by or against a child
  - ○ Consent judgment in a claim for provisional damages that has settled pre-commencement
  - ○ A trustee is seeking guidance from the court
- ➢ Part 8 is required by a rule or PD

Content

Part 8 claims must state:
- ➢ That Part 8 applies
- ➢ The question C would like the court to decide, or the remedy C seeks with the legal basis, and
- ➢ If C is claiming under an enactment, that enactment

C must file and serve any written evidence relied upon, but Particulars of Claim are not required.

Responding to Part 8 claims

D acknowledges service, stating:
- ➢ Whether D contests the claim
- ➢ If D seeks a different remedy, and
- ➢ If D contends Part 8 should not be used, why not

4.3. Methods of service within the jurisdiction

There are 7 different methods of service within the jurisdiction set out in CPR 6. They are:
- ➢ By the court
- ➢ Personal service
- ➢ By Post or DX
- ➢ By leaving at a place
- ➢ Contractually agreed methods
- ➢ Electronic methods (fax and email)
- ➢ Other methods authorised by the court

Service by the court

This is the normal method. C must notify the court if C wishes to serve the Claim Form. The court will serve by first class post.

Where the court serves by post, and the Claim Form is returned[11]
> ➤ The court notifies C that form has been returned, and
> ➤ The Claim Form is deemed to be served

Personal service

C personally serves D by giving D the Claim Form. The person C needs to give the form to depends on the identity of D:

Identity of D	Who C serves form on
D an individual	That individual
D a company	Person who holds a senior position in company, e.g director / treasurer / manager / CEO
D a partnership	Partner or controller / manager of partnership

(Refer to the table at Chapter 4.7 for the place of service)

Personal service is disallowed where:
> ➤ D acts by solicitor and has given an address for service[12], or
> ➤ C brings proceedings against the Crown

First class post or DX

C may choose to serve D himself by first class post or DX (a delivery service).

Leaving Claim Form at a specified place

C may serve D by leaving the Claim Form at:
> ➤ D's solicitor's address for service

---

[11] CPR 6.18
[12] CPR 6.7

> An address nominated by D for service, or
> D's usual or last known residence
>> o (for the place of residence where D is not a natural person, see Chapter 4.7 below)

If C does not know D's usual or last known residence, or if C suspects it is not current, then:
> C must take reasonable steps to ascertain the current residence and serve there, else
> C must make an application to the court to serve by an alternative method or at an alternative place, else
> C may serve on last known residence

Contractually agreed method
If C and D have agreed a method through contract then C can serve D by following that method.

Electronic service: fax or email
In order to serve D electronically, D must have previously indicated that D will accept service by fax or email.

D must have given the indication in writing providing the number or address. The following are sufficient:
> Fax number on headed paper
> Email address on headed paper with express permission to serve by email
> Fax number or email address on a statement of case

C must ask D if there are any limitations to D's agreement to accept service.

Court authorised alternative methods
As noted above, C may make an application to the court to authorise an alternative method of service.

4.4. Deemed service

Claim Forms

Claim Forms are deemed served on the second business day after the completion of the relevant step for service: CPR 6.14. For example, a Claim Form posted on Monday is deemed served on Wednesday.

Other documents: CPR 6.26

The date of deemed service for other documents depends on the method.

Method	Deemed served
First class post or DX	Second day after posting, provided that day is a business day.
Delivery Fax or email Personal service	If before 4.30pm on a business day, that day. If after 4.30pm, the next business day.

See the examples at PD 6A [10].

4.5. Validity and renewal of Claim Forms

Time limit for service after issue

A Claim Form must be served on D, with a Particulars of Claim, within 4 months of issuing the Claim Form: CPR 7.5.

Application to extend time: CPR 7.6

In order to extend the time for service of a Claim Form C must have acted promptly.

The court will exercise its discretion to extend time where:
> The court itself has failed to serve the Claim Form, or
> C has taken all reasonable steps to serve but has not been able

C must usually make the application within the time limit, supported by evidence, and state:[13]

- ➤ All the circumstances relied upon
- ➤ The date of issue
- ➤ The expiry date for service
- ➤ A full explanation

The application can be made without notice.

4.6. Bringing and settling proceedings by or against children or mentally incapable persons: CPR 21

Special rules apply if C brings a claim against a child or a protected party.

Children
The Claim Form must be served on:
- ➤ One of the child's parents / guardians, or otherwise
- ➤ The adult with whom the child resides

This rule does not apply where the court allows proceedings without a litigation friend.

Protected Parties
The Claim Form must be served on:
- ➤ A person with power of attorney, or
- ➤ A person appointed by Court of Protection, otherwise
- ➤ An adult with whom the protected party resides

Unlike the discretion the court possesses regarding children, a protected party **must** have a litigation friend to conduct proceedings on his behalf.

C may always apply to serve on a different party.

---

[13] PD 7A [8]

4.7. Bringing proceedings by or against legal persons, charities and trusts, deceased persons and bankrupts

Place of service: legal persons

The place where C serves D depends on the status of D:

Identity of D	Where C serves
D a sole trader	➤ Usual or last known residence of the individual, or ➤ Last known place of business
D a partnership	➤ Usual or last known residence of the individual, or ➤ Last known place of business
D a company	➤ Principal office of the company, or ➤ Any place of business of the company which has a real connection with the claim
D a LPP	➤ Principal office of the LPP, or ➤ Any place of business of the LPP which has a real connection with the claim

Charities and trusts

Trustees, executors and administrators should act jointly. All should be named in any proceedings (as Ds if they will not consent to act as Cs).

A claim may be brought by or against trustees, executors or administrators without the need to join the beneficiaries.[14]

Deceased persons

If a person has a claim and dies before bringing the claim, the claim vests in the deceased's personal representatives.[15] The personal representatives should be named as parties in any litigation.

If a claim is brought against someone who was dead when the claim was issued it will be treated as if it was brought against the estate of the deceased.

---

[14] CPR 19.7A [1]
[15] Apart from a defamation claim

Bankrupts

When a person becomes bankrupt their estate vests in the trustee in bankruptcy. There is an exception for PI and defamation claims, which remain vested in the bankrupt. The trustee should be named in litigation against the estate. Proceedings against a bankrupt may only be commenced with the court's permission.

The bankrupt person is not able to make applications in litigation.

CHAPTER SUMMARY
- ➤ Part 7 claims are the normal type of claim.
- ➤ After a claim is issued it must be served within 4 months.
- ➤ Service by the court by first class post is the normal method of service.

5. PROCEEDINGS INVOLVING THREE OR MORE PARTIES AND MULTIPLE CAUSES OF ACTION

Litigation may involve more than one C and D. Additional parties may bring related but different claims that arise from the same facts. Joining the litigation together allows the courts to achieve a consistent outcome whilst hopefully saving both time and cost.

5.1. Multiple causes of action: CPR 7.3

Where multiple causes of action exist a single Claim Form should be used to start all claims that can be conveniently disposed of in the same proceedings.

5.2. Multiple parties

Where multiple persons hold the same right they must all be joined as Cs. If they will not consent to being joined as Cs they should be added as Ds.

Where liability is joint but not several then every person jointly liable must be made a D.

Group litigation: CPR 19.11 and PD 19B
Where a number of claims give rise to common or related issues of fact or law, those claims can be joined in one set of proceedings.

5.3. Addition and substitution of parties

Addition of a new party: CPR 19.2(2)
The court may order a new party (an 'intervener') to be added where:
> The presence of an intervener is desirable to ensure all matters in dispute can be resolved, or
> An issue exists between the intervener and an existing party that is connected with a matter in dispute and it is desirable to determine this issue at the same time

If proceedings have already been served an intervener needs the permission of the court to be added as a party.

Substitution of an existing party for a new party: CPR 19.2(4)
The court may order the substitution of an existing party for a new party where:
> ➤ The existing party's interest has passed to the new party, and
> ➤ It is desirable for the substitution to occur to resolve the matters in dispute

As with interveners, if proceedings have already been served, the permission of the court is required for a substitution to occur.

An application for substitution can be made without notice but it must be supported by evidence.

For the addition of substitution of parties after the expiry of limitation, see Chapter 10.5.

5.4. Additional claims: CPR 20

An additional claim is a claim brought by a party other than C following C's claim. There are three types of additional claims:[16]
> ➤ **Type 1:** Counterclaim by D against C or against another person
> ➤ **Type 2:** Additional claim by D against another person (who may or may not currently be a party)
> ➤ **Type 3:** Additional claim by a new party: CPR 20.7

The management of these claims is illustrated in the diagram over the next page.

With the exception of counterclaims, all additional claims are brought using Part 20. A Part 20 claim is to be treated as a claim for the purposes of the CPR.

---

[16] CPR 20.2(1)

Formal requirements

A Part 20 claim must include:

- ➤ The main claim number
- ➤ Details of C and D
- ➤ Brief details of the additional claim
- ➤ A statement of value
- ➤ The name and address of TP
- ➤ Particulars of Claim
- ➤ A statement of truth

The CPR 10 rules on acknowledgment of service do not apply to a C defending a CC. The CPR 12 default judgment rules are not applicable to additional claims by a D or by a new party claiming additionally (the second and third types of additional claim).

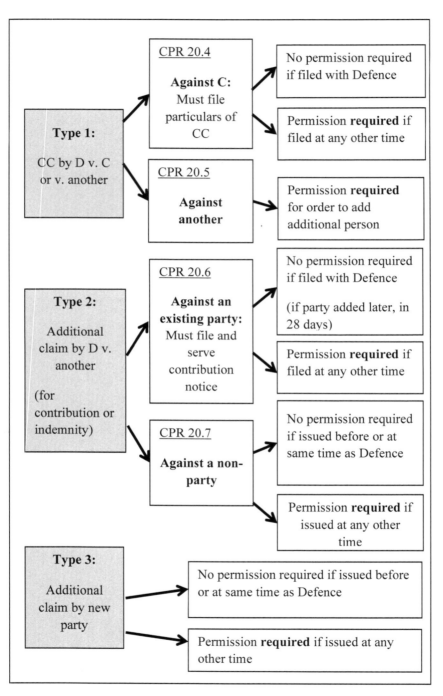

Type 1:

CC by D v. C or v. another

CPR 20.4

Against C: Must file particulars of CC

No permission required if filed with Defence

Permission **required** if filed at any other time

CPR 20.5

Against another

Permission **required** for order to add additional person

Type 2:

Additional claim by D v. another

(for contribution or indemnity)

CPR 20.6

Against an existing party: Must file and serve contribution notice

No permission required if filed with Defence

(if party added later, in 28 days)

Permission **required** if filed at any other time

CPR 20.7

Against a non-party

No permission required if issued before or at same time as Defence

Permission **required** if issued at any other time

Type 3:

Additional claim by new party

No permission required if issued before or at same time as Defence

Permission **required** if issued at any other time

5.5. Effect on additional claims if main proceedings determined without trial

An additional claim is treated as a separate claim. Therefore, determination of the main claim (by settlement, dismissal or strike out) will not always lead to the determination of the additional claim.

However, whether there will then be any point continuing the additional claim will depend on the type of relief sought.

For example, if D claims an indemnity or contribution from a TP and the main claim is dismissed or struck out, there will be no need for the additional claim. However, if the main claim is settled, the question of contribution or indemnification remains. Therefore, the additional claim may continue.

CHAPTER SUMMARY
> Different rules apply depending on who is bringing the additional claim and who it is against.
> The underlying purpose of Part 20 is to enable additional claims to be managed in the most convenient and cost effective manner, avoiding divergent judgments.

6. STATEMENTS OF CASE

Certain key documents are designated 'statements of case'. Additional rules apply to these documents.

6.1. Documents designated statements of case: CPR 2.3

The following documents are statements of case:
- ➢ Claim Form
- ➢ Particulars of Claim
- ➢ Defence
- ➢ Counterclaim
- ➢ Reply
- ➢ Additional (Part 20) claims
- ➢ Response to a Part 18 request for further information

6.2. Form of a statement of case: PD 5A

A document that is a statement of case must:[17]
- ➢ Not be more than 25 pages long, and
- ➢ Be printed on durable quality A4 paper, and
- ➢ Have margins of 35 mm, and
- ➢ Be bound, typed and legible

6.3. Content of a statement of case: CPR 16.2 [1]

Part 7 claims must state in their Claim Form and Particulars of Claim:[18]
- ➢ A concise statement of the nature of the claim, and
- ➢ The remedy sought, and
- ➢ The address

If C is making a money claim, C must give a statement of value, either:[19]
- ➢ The amount claimed, or
- ➢ Amount for allocation (< £10k, £10k – £25k, £25k+), or

---

[17] And indeed any document to be filed with the court
[18] CPR 16.2
[19] CPR 16.2. Disregard interest, costs, CN, CC and benefits in assessment

> Whether C cannot say how much C expects to recover
> (If the claim is for PI, C must state whether the value of the claim is < £1k or > £1k)

If the claim is for a specified sum, C must include a statement of interest on that sum. C must state the basis for claiming interest.

If the claim is in the High Court, C must:
> State that value of the claim is > £100k (for PI claims > £50k), and
> State which list C would like the case to be in

If the claim is for PI, C must give:
> C's date of birth, and
> Details of the injuries, and
> Schedule of past and future losses, and
> Medical report if relying upon one, and
> If C's condition may worsen

A party may:
> Refer to any point of law on which their claim is based, and
> Serve any documents that the party thinks necessary

6.4. Statements of truth: CPR 22

Statements of truth are required for every statement of case. If they are not given then:[20]
> The party may not rely upon the statement of case as evidence of the matters set out in it
> The court may strike out the statement of case
> The innocent party can apply to strike out the statement of case

The consequence of verifying a document with a statement of truth without honest belief in its truth is contempt of court.[21] Proceedings for

---

[20] CPR 22.2
[21] CPR 32.14

37

contempt may only be brought with the permission of the court or Attorney General.

6.5. Responding to a statement of case

Timeline

The normal timeline of litigation is as follows:

Step	Time
C issues a Claim Form with court	C has 4 months in which to serve the Claim Form (see Chapter 4.5).
Court serves Claim Form on D	C has 14 days to serve Particulars of Claim on D.[22]
C serves Particulars of Claim on D	D has 14 days to file an AoS or a Defence.
D files an Acknowledgement of Service	If D files an AoS, D has 28 days **from receipt of the Particular of Claim** to file a Defence.
D files a Defence	D may make a **counterclaim** in his Defence.
Court will send parties notice of a provisional allocation	Depending on the track, parties have 14 or 28 days to complete directions questionnaire. See Chapter 1.4.
Parties complete directions questionnaire. C may file a **Reply** to D's Defence.	A Reply is optional.

Parties may also make applications for further information (see Chapter 11).

Requirement to respond in a Defence[23]

A party who fails to respond to an allegation in their Defence will be taken to admit that allegation. However, if D has set out the nature of her defence in her case, D will be taken to require proof of the

---

[22] Particulars of Claim could be included with the Claim Form
[23] CPR 16.5

allegation. In a money claim, unless D expressly admits the amount, D will be taken as requiring proof of the amount.

If denying an allegation, reasons must be given. If a different version of events is relied upon, that version of events must be given.

Replies

By contrast to Defences, replies are optional. A failure to reply is taken as requiring proof. Replies should not be inconsistent with the Particulars of Claim.

CHAPTER SUMMARY

> Every statement of case requires a statement of truth.
> Ds must respond to allegations in their Defence but Replies are optional.

7. REMEDIES

Although often relegated to a mere week on most contract courses and completely overlooked in courses on torts and equity, remedies are of crucial importance to the practitioner.

7.1. Cost of pursuing a remedy

Litigation is time consuming and expensive. Despite costs-shifting (see Chapter 22.3) parties will almost never recover all of their costs or time. Parties must weigh the cost of pursuing a remedy when deciding whether or not to embark in litigation.

7.2. Availability of self-help remedies

A self-help remedy is a legal remedy that a party can exercise without the need for a court order. The cost of pursuing a remedy through the courts means that 'self-help' remedies are extremely valuable. The most important self-help remedy is **termination** for a repudiatory breach of contract.

7.3. Availability of ADR

ADR is always available if the parties are willing to engage in it. Both parties must agree to ADR. Sometimes this agreement is obtained through contract in advance of any dispute. Such a contract may require ADR and a party who fails to comply will be in breach of contract.

The cost and speed of ADR varies greatly depending on the method chosen.

7.4. Capacity of D to pay damages

Before pursuing a remedy a party should think carefully about the capacity of their potential D to pay damages. An impecunious D will not be able to pay damages nor costs and C will lose more money pursuing the claim.

D may be insured, or there may be an alternative, a wealthier D may be available, such as a bank.

7.5. Pursuing a range of remedies

It will often be the case that a range of remedies is open to a party. English law allows parties to claim for all available remedies and then, after judgment, choose the most advantageous remedies (although remedies inconsistent with each other cannot be chosen). It will therefore almost always be in a party's interest to pursue the full range of remedies.

7.6. Pursuing interim remedies

In addition to pursuing final remedies a party may wish to apply for an interim remedy. This may mitigate against the delay of litigation but can require an expensive undertaking (see further Chapters 17 and 18).

7.7. Applicable time limits

Some remedies may be barred through limitation (see Chapter 3) or similar doctrines such as laches. For example, the remedy of rescission for misrepresentation (see Chapter 8) can be barred through lapse of time. It is important to consider whether any remedies are, or will soon become, time barred.

CHAPTER SUMMARY
> Prior to commencing litigation parties should consider both ADR and self-help remedies.
> Prospective Cs should investigate whether a prospective D will be able to pay damages if C does ultimately obtain judgment.

8. CONTRACT

A range of remedies are available against a contract-breaker. The normal remedy is damages.

8.1. Damages: general principles

If a contract has been breached damages are available **as of right**. The core principle underlying the award is to **compensate** C for his loss. The general rule is that damages are assessed at the time of the breach.

C's entitlement to damages may be calculated by either:
1. The expectation interest, or
2. The reliance interest

Expectation Interest

> This is the normal measure of damages. The damages are 'forward looking' and intended to put C into the position in which she would have been if the contract had been performed

> This includes both loss of promised performance and the loss of profit resulting from not being able to put the performance to use. In either case the loss cannot be too remote

Reliance Interest

> The reliance interest is the amount that C has lost in reliance on the contract that has been breached. It is used when C cannot show what C would have lost, but only what C has lost

> C cannot use the reliance measure if the contract would have been a bad bargain

8.2. Limitations on compensatory damages

Remoteness of loss

The loss sustained by C cannot be too remote. Under *Hadley v Baxendale*,[24] this means that the loss must be in the reasonable contemplation of both parties. Traditionally, the court allowed losses that:

> ➤ Flowed naturally from the breach, or
> ➤ Were contemplated as a serious possibility by both parties

The approach set out in *The Achilleas*[25] instead asks what the parties intended the scope of recoverable losses to be. It seems that the two approaches do not produce greatly different results.

C's duty to mitigate loss

The general rule is that C is required to take reasonable steps to reduce her loss and to avoid taking action that may increase the loss suffered.

Damages for distress / disappointment

The general rule is that damages for distress or disappointment are not available following a breach of contract.[26] However, where the purpose of the contract is C's enjoyment or to prevent C's distress, damages can be sought for a breach. An example is a contract for a holiday. However, the amount of the award is usually limited to £10,000.[27]

8.3. The availability of equitable remedies

Although damages are C's primary remedy following a breach of contract C may also seek equitable remedies. Equitable remedies are at the discretion of the court.

---

[24] [1854] 9 Ex 341
[25] [2008] UKHL 48
[26] *Addis v Gramophone Co Ltd* [1909] AC 488
[27] *Farley v Skinner* [2001] 3 WLR 899

Specific performance

Specific performance is an order of the court requiring a party to a contract to perform or complete the performance of her contractual obligations.

Before a court will consider ordering specific performance C must show that damages would be inadequate as a remedy. This requires C to demonstrate the uniqueness of the thing contracted for and the ineffectiveness of damages to compensate C, for example, the sale of a Ming vase.

Specific performance is unlikely to be granted for contracts requiring supervision, building contracts or contracts for a personal service. It will similarly be refused if the order would cause severe hardship to D.[28]

Injunctions

The court possesses the equitable jurisdiction to order D to do or not do a specific act. A mandatory injunction requires D to do an act and a prohibitory injunction requires D not to do an act. Mandatory orders are generally harder to obtain from a court than prohibitory orders. An injunction can be either final or interim (refer to Chapter 18).

An injunction for breach of contract may be ordered in support of C's contractual rights or following an actual or threatened breach by D. Where a breach is merely threatened, a higher degree of proof will be required.

Rescission

If a contract is rescinded it is set aside and the parties are restored to the position they would have been in had the contract never been made. Rescission is a 'self-help' remedy (see Chapter 7.2).

In the contractual context, rescission is available in three situations:
- ➢ Misrepresentation
- ➢ Undue influence
- ➢ Duress

---

[28] *Co-operative Insurance Society Ltd v Argyll Stores (Holdings) Ltd* [1998] AC 1

There are four equitable limits to rescission:
- ➤ *Restitutio in integrum* is not possible (that is, the parties cannot be returned to their original positions prior to entering the contract)
- ➤ A TP has acquired rights for value without notice in relation to the contract and is therefore protected by the court as 'equity's darling'
- ➤ C has affirmed the contract
- ➤ There has been an unreasonable delay by C between discovering the serious breach and seeking to rescind the contract

Rectification

The terms of a contract agreed by the parties may be incorrectly set down in a document purporting to contain the full terms of the contract. In such a situation the court may order the correction of that document to reflect the true agreement.

Rectification becomes a potential remedy where there has been a mistake by both parties in recording the contract. Clear evidence is required.

Rectification is subject to similar equitable limits as rescission.

8.4. Remedies for misrepresentation

There are multiple causes of action available with regard to misrepresentation. Not all are based in contract:

D's culpability	Cause of action	Remedy
Innocent	Misrepresentation in equity	Rescission
Negligent	Tort of negligence	Damages for reasonably foreseeable losses
Negligent	Statutory tort in s 2(1) Misrepresentation Act 1967	Damages for all losses
Fraudulent	Tort of deceit	Damages for all losses

Further, the statement that was a misrepresentation may have been included as a term, or been a contract in itself. In such a case damages for breach of contract, or breach of a collateral warranty will be available. Such damages will put C in the position had the statement been true (the 'expectation interest').

Damages in lieu of rescission
The court has the power to order damages 'in lieu' of rescission under s 2(2) Misrepresentation Act 1967. Instead of rescinding the contract, the court will award damages. The damages should not exceed the expectation interest.

8.5. The law and practice in respect of interest on judgment debts pursuant to contract or statute

Courts have the discretion to award interest on all or any part of damages awarded for all or any part of the period from the date of the cause of action until the date of payment or judgment.[29]

The interest charged on judgment debts is entirely **distinct** from that charged on damages.

Interest on damages is there to compensate for loss of use of the money that C would have otherwise had. Interest on judgment debt is to

---

[29] s 69 County Courts Act 1984 and s 35A Senior Courts Act 1981

encourage payment of that judgment debt as close to the date of judgment being given as possible. The general rule is that interest runs from the date judgment is given.[30]

If a contract between C and D fixes an agreed interest rate on judgment debts the court has no power to fix a different rate.

If no such contractual arrangement exists then the courts possess statutory powers to charge interest on a judgment debt as shown in the table overleaf.

Statute	Interest rate	Application
County Court (Interest on Judgment Debts) Order 1991	8%	All county court judgments over £5000
Judgments Act 1838	8%	All High Court judgments
Late Payments of Commercial Debts (Interest) Act 1998	8% above the official dealing rate at the last 30 June or 31 December (0.5% at time of writing)	Contracts to which this Act applies

CHAPTER SUMMARY

➤ Damages in contract are normally aimed at putting C into the position she would have been in had the contract been performed.

➤ There are different causes of action available for different types of misrepresentation that give different remedies.

➤ Interest on damages is distinct from interest on judgment debts.

---

[30] CPR 40.8(1)

47

9. TORT

Although the general principles of quantifying damages in tort are straightforward care is needed in the application of those principles to cases of PI.

9.1. General principles

Compensatory
Damages in tort are aimed at putting the victim back in the position that she should have been in had the tort not been committed.[31] They are designed to compensate the victim for her loss.

Reduction of damages
Some losses may be too remote to be recoverable.[32] Damages in tort may be also be reduced by contributory negligence (CN) or D's failure to mitigate.

Aggravated damages
Additional 'aggravated' damages may be awarded in tort. They are primarily compensatory and are awarded when D's conduct is especially reprehensible and causes C a special loss.

Exemplary damages
Additional 'exemplary' damages may also be awarded in tort. The justification for exemplary damages is much disputed. There are three categories where they can be awarded:[33]
- ➤ Oppressive, arbitrary or unconstitutional actions by servants of the Government
- ➤ When D's conduct was calculated to make a profit beyond C's compensation
- ➤ When expressly authorised by statute

---

[31] Damages in tort are often contrasted to damages in contract, which are usually aimed at putting C in the position C would have been in had the contract been performed
[32] In the tort of negligence: *The Wagon Mound* [1961] UKPC 1
[33] *Rookes v Barnard* [1964] AC 1129

Availability of injunctions

Injunctions can be sought to prevent continuous torts. A final injunction has been described as the 'prima facie remedy' in the torts of nuisance and trespass. Further, a *quia timet* injunction may be available where there is imminent danger of irreparable harm. The detailed law on the availability of injunctions is outside the scope of this book.

Provisional damages: s 32A Senior Court Act 1981

Provisional damages are available when it is proved or admitted that there is a chance that in the future C will suffer a serious deterioration or develop a serious disease. C is given an initial award of general damages that is lower than a once-and-for-all award, with the possibility of making a future claim if the tort does occur.

9.2. Quantification: five step overview

Quantification of damages in a PI claim can be reduced to the five steps below.

Step 1: Add up all special damages

Definition

Special damages are damages capable of quantification in terms of money, for example medical expenses or a broken watch. Only what can be proved and what has been reasonably incurred will be recoverable and therefore special damages can only be awarded for losses incurred up until date of trial.

Loss of earnings

The most important special damages are historic loss of earnings. C's claim is for the lost earnings as a result of the tort. It can include loss of the chance (for example, of being promoted). Conversely, there can be deductions (for example, if C was due to retire).

Usually C will have a regular income that can be used to calculate the loss. Where earnings fluctuate an average of the last 6 – 10 pay packets can be taken. Lost earnings are calculated net of tax, compulsory pension payments and expenses (for example, travel costs).

Other categories of special damages are the cost of a new home, loss of a company care and loss of unpaid care by a relative but space precludes detailed coverage here.

Step 2: Add up all general damages

Definition
General damages are damages not capable of quantification in terms of money. They include PSLA, future expenses and **future loss of earnings**.

PSLA
The valuation of PSLA is conventional. Tables categorise and quantify different forms of loss. Medical evidence will assist the court in determining the valuation. As a result of the Jackson reforms, general damages were **increased by 10%** from 2013.[34]

Future loss of earnings
Future lost earnings are calculated using the formula:

$$Multiplicand \times Multiplier$$

C's net annual loss of earnings is the 'multiplicand'. The number of years that C would have worked is the 'multiplier'. The multiplier is based on the Ogden tables that predict the number of years in work remaining for a hypothetical person of a given sex, using their current and likely retirement age.

There is a 3% discount rate (as C is assumed to invest her award) and a discount for contingencies. If C would have been promoted, there are two options. The first is to increase the multiplicand to represent an average higher net earnings and use a single multiplier. The second is to use two separate multipliers for the pre- and post-promotion periods.

Future expenses that would be reasonably recoverable if they had already been incurred will be recoverable.

---

[34] *Simmons v Castle* [2012] EWCA Civ 1039

Other categories of general damages are lost years, loss of earning capacity and loss of pension rights but space precludes detailed coverage here.

Step 3: Deduct contributory negligence

Once a total amount of damages has been calculated, CN is deducted.

Step 4: Deduct recoverable Social Security payments

It will often be the case that a C has received Social Security payments after suffering a tort. C should not be able to recover twice (once via the benefits system and once via D).

When D pays damages to C, D will first pay the Government an amount equal to the benefits recoverable from C. D will then deduct that amount from the damages paid to C. Deductions may only be from the relevant head (so Job Seekers' Allowance is deducted from lost earnings) and cannot reduce C's compensation below zero.

The major benefits are recoverable although not all are. Benevolent donations to a victim are not deducted.

Step 5: Interest on damages in PI claims: s 35A Senior Courts Act 1981, s 69 County Courts Act 1984

Special damages
Interest is awarded from the date of the tort to the date of trial. The rate is fixed and is currently 0.5%.

General damages
Interest is awarded from date of service of the Claim Form until date of trial. The rate is 2%.

9.3. Practical advice: structured settlement

As a practical step the parties can agree that damages will not be paid as a lump sum but instead in a structured settlement. Payments will be made annually on an ongoing basis and in future lump sums. Such settlements can give increased flexibility to both parties but are simply an alternative method of paying (as opposed to quantifying) damages.

CHAPTER SUMMARY
> The basic principle underlying damages in tort is to put C into the position she would have been in had the wrong not been committed.
> Future earnings are a type of general damages.

10. AMENDMENT

Developments in the information available to parties in a case as well as the discovery of errors in drafting mean that statements of case may need to be updated as proceedings continue. The CPR supports the amendment of statements of case so as to ensure the main issues in dispute can be established and categorically answered by the court.

10.1. Permission to amend

When permission or consent is required: CPR 17.1
A party may amend their statement of case at any time **before** it has been served on any other party without seeking permission or consent.

However, if a statement of case has been **served**, a party may amend only:
> With the written consent of all the other parties, or
> With the permission of the court

Seeking permission: PD 17 [1.1 - 1.2]
When making an application to amend a statement of case an applicant should file an application notice and a copy of the statement of case with the proposed amendments.

The application will then be dealt with at a hearing. It may be dealt with on the papers if the parties consent or if the court considers it unnecessary to hold a hearing.

Power of court to disallow amendments: CPR 17.2
If a party has amended their statement of case where permission of the court was not required the court may disallow the amendment.
If the opposing party seeks to challenge an amendment they must apply within 14 days of service of the amended statements of case.

10.2. Principles governing applications for permission to amend: PD 17 [1.1 – 1.5]

Neither CPR 17.1 nor PD 17[1] offer specific guidance on how a court will exercise its discretion when assessing whether to allow an amendment. The court will therefore be guided by the overriding objective at CPR 1.1.

The court will consider whether it is just and at proportionate cost to allow the amendment of a statement of case. This will often depend on the **stage** at which an amendment is sought. For example, a court is unlikely to allow a late amendment to a statement of case that introduces drastic changes from the original filed and served version. On the other hand, an amended draft statement of case purely seeking to clarify information or an issue at an early stage is likely to be allowed.

10.3. New causes of action after the expiry of limitation: CPR 17.4

Amendments after the expiry of limitation: CPR 17.4(2) – (4)
The court may allow an amendment:
> That will add or substitute a new claim but only if the new claim arises out of the same facts or substantially the same facts as a claim already made,[35] or
> To correct a mistake as to the name of a party, but only where the mistake was genuine, or
> To alter the capacity in which a party claims if the new capacity is one that that party had when the proceedings started or has since acquired

---

[35] s 35(4) Limitation Act 1980

Two stage test: CPR 17.4.4

The burden is on the applicant to demonstrate that the amendment falls within CPR 17.4.

If a party seeks to amend their statement of case in order to add or substitute a new claim after the limitation period has expired the court asks:

1. Whether the amendment would involve the addition or substitution of a new cause of action. **If it would not**, the court has the discretion to allow the amendment.

2. **If the amendment would add or substitute a new cause of action**: the court asks whether the new cause of action arise out of the same facts or substantially the same facts as those already pleaded. If it would not, the court may not allow the amendment.

10.4. Adding or substituting parties after the expiry of limitation: CPR 19.5

In addition to seeking amendment to add or substitute a new claim, an applicant may seek to add or substitute a new party under CPR 19.5(2) – (3).

A court may order addition / substitution where:

➤ The relevant limitation period (see Chapter 3) was current when the proceedings were originally started, **and**

➤ The addition / substitution is 'necessary', which includes where:

   o There has been a mistake of nomenclature or identification in naming a party, or

   o The claim cannot progress without addition/substitution of a new party, or

   o The original party has died or is bankrupt, and his interest has passed to the new party

If the above conditions can all be satisfied, the court will decide whether to exercise its discretion to allow the amendment. The court will exercise that discretion in accordance with the overriding objective in CPR 1.1. Since the post-Jackson reform requirement of 'at proportionate cost' is now included in CPR 1.1(1) alongside 'justly', the expense and delay caused by the amendment is likely to be an increasingly prominent consideration for the courts.

10.5. Amendments affecting accrued limitation rights

A court will **not** grant D permission to amend D's statement of case where the effect of such an amendment would be to transfer responsibility for the claim on to a new party who cannot be sued by C because C would be time-barred.

However, if C knew of the facts indicating the new party could be sued prior to commencing proceedings, D may be allowed to amend since C has effectively elected to not pursue the proposed new party. The fact that C will be time-barred against the new party will be to C's prejudice.

10.6. Costs consequences of amending

The general rule is that where an amendment is allowed, the party seeking to amend must pay the other side's consequential costs of the amendment. Those cost include the costs relating to the application itself, the preparation for the application, and the knock-on amendments of other statements of case.

If C seeks to make reasonable amendments to a statement of case at an early stage of proceedings, D (and all other parties) should consider giving their consent. An unreasonable refusal to consent may result in the loss of the usual costs orders against the party applying to amend.

If C seeks to make an amendment to a statement of case at a very late stage of proceedings and the court is persuaded to allow it, C may be faced with particularly onerous costs orders. Therefore, costs considerations will remain central to the question of whether C should amend.

➤ A party should seek the consent of other parties before seeking the permission of the court. This may save the cost of making an application.

➤ CPR 17 and PD 17 offer little guidance as to how a court should exercise its discretion when faced with an application to amend. Resort is made to the overriding objective in CPR 1.1.

➤ Permission is not needed to amend a statement of case that has not yet been served.

11. FURTHER INFORMATION

There is never a case in which there is not some further information or clarification, which a party could seek. The question is whether one should ask for it. This requires an awareness of tactical considerations and costs.

11.1. When it may be appropriate to make a request for further information

Under CPR 18.1 the court has the power (following an application or on its own initiative) to order a party to clarify or give additional information. That party must then file a response and serve it on all the other parties.

The first party (seeking further information) should make a preliminary request to the second party (responding) before approaching the court. That preliminary request should be restricted to what is **necessary and proportionate**.

PD 18 [1.1 – 1.7] offers guidelines on making preliminary requests.

If a preliminary request is unsuccessful, it may then become appropriate to apply for an order under CPR 18.1.

PD 18 [5.1 – 5.8] offers guidelines on making applications for such orders.

Part 18 requests do not apply to the small claims track, although the court may order a party to clarify its case.

11.2. Principles when allowing requests for further information

Following an application for an order under CPR 18.1 the Court has the discretion to make the order. It must have regard to:[36]
  ➤ The likely benefit which will result from the new information

---

[36] CPR 18.1.5

> The likely cost of giving the information
> Whether the financial resources of the second party are sufficient to enable compliance with the order

11.3. How to respond to a request for further information: PD 18 [2.1 – 2.4]

A response to a request must be:
> In writing
> Dated
> Signed by the responding party or his representative
> Verified by a statement of truth[37]

Where the request is by letter the responding party may respond in a letter or by formal reply. If by letter, the letter must be clearly identified as a response to the request. It must not contain any other unrelated matter. The response becomes a statement of case.

Unless the responding party responds on the same document, PD 18 requires a response to repeat each element of the request and then set out the response below in a question / answer format.

When the responding party serves a copy on every other party it must serve a copy of the request and the response on the court.

CHAPTER SUMMARY
> Before making an application for a CPR 18.1 order the party should first make a preliminary request.
> A court can make an order for further information of its own initiative.
> The usual way to set out a response is in a question / answer format.

---

[37] PD 18 [3]

12. Interim Applications

An interim application is an application made by a party to proceedings between commencement and trial. Some interim applications are made to enforce judgments after a trial. The rules governing applications for court orders are found in CPR 23 and PD 23.

In this chapter an Applicant 'A' makes an interim application that a Respondent 'R' opposes.

12.1. With notice and without notice applications

An application to the court made with notice provides R with the opportunity to respond to submissions by A at the hearing.

In contrast, an application without notice is made by A to the judge without R present. Any interim order made at a without notice hearing should make provision for a return date where both A and R may make submissions.

The general rule is that an application notice must be served on each R. However, under PD 23A [3], an application may only be made without serving an application notice:[38]
- ➢ Where there is exceptional urgency,
- ➢ Where the overriding objective is best furthered by doing so,
- ➢ By consent of all parties,
- ➢ With the permission of the court, or
- ➢ Where a court order, rule or PD permits

A without notice application may be warranted if there are good reasons for not giving notice, such as the immediacy of the remedy sought or the initial confidentiality of the issue concerned.[39] Once an order is made without notice, A is under a duty to serve the respondent with all the relevant documents from the hearing.[40]

---

[38] CPR 23.4 and PD 23A [3]
[39] CPR 25.3(1)
[40] CPR 23.9

12.2. Documentation required in interim applications

The general rule is that an interim application for a court order must be made by an **application notice**.[41] A rule, PD or court order may dispense with the requirement for an application notice.

An application notice must contain or be accompanied by:[42]
> What order A is seeking
> Why A is seeking that order
> Any supporting witness statement, and
> A draft order

12.3. Calculating notice periods: PD 23A [4.1 – 4.2]

An application notice must be served as soon as practicable after it has been issued. If there is to be a hearing the application notice must be served **at least 3 clear days** before the hearing date.[43]

Where an application notice should be served but there is not sufficient time to do so, **informal notification** of the application should be given unless the circumstances of the application require secrecy.

CPR 2.8(2) – (3) offers guidance on the exact definition of 'days' for the purpose of calculation.

12.4. Duty of full and frank disclosure in without notice applications

This duty applies to all without notice applications. It requires A to reveal all material facts even if those facts may weaken A's case.

The underlying rationale behind this duty is to ensure a judge at an interim application does not grant an interim order based on a one-sided presentation of an issue. This saves the court time.

---

[41] CPR 23.3
[42] CPR 23.6
[43] For a telephone hearing: at least 5 clear days must be given

CHAPTER SUMMARY

➢ <u>CPR 23</u> application notices are the normal way of making an application to the court.

➢ An application notice is normally required for any application.

13. Judgment without trial

The court does not decide every case after a trial. Parties may apply for judgment without a trial where:
- ➢ No Defence has been filed (Default Judgment)
- ➢ No trial is needed (Summary Judgment)

Default Judgment: CPR 12

13.1. Availability of default judgment

Default judgment is generally available, unless:
- ➢ The claim is for delivery of goods subject to the Consumer Credit Act 1974
- ➢ The Part 8 procedure is used, or
- ➢ The claim is an admiralty, arbitration, contentious probate, provisional damages or possession claim

The amount awarded in a default judgment will be the amount claimed by C in the Particulars of Claim. If C is claiming an unspecified amount the court will decide the amount. Judgment may be given for interest if interest has been claimed.

13.2. Time for entry of default judgment

Default judgment will be entered against D if D has not filed an Acknowledgment of Service ('AoS') or a Defence in the relevant time.

The relevant time begins after C serves D with a Particulars of Claim. D has 14 days to file either an AoS. If D files an AoS, D then has 28 days from receipt of the Particulars of Claim to file a Defence. Refer to the table at Chapter 6.5 for a timeline.

D may alternatively **admit** that C has a valid claim or simply comply with (**'satisfy'**) C's claim.

13.3. Procedure for default judgment

If C is entitled to default judgment then C will make either a **request or an application**. A request requires an administrative act of the court. An application is made to a judge.

C will make a request for default judgment in a specified or unspecified money claim. In claims for all other remedies C will make an application by <u>Part 23</u> (see Chapter 12.2). C must:
  - ➢ Show that the Particulars of Claim were served. A certificate of service on the court file will be sufficient
  - ➢ Show that D has not filed an AoS / Defence / admission / satisfied C's claim, and
  - ➢ Prove D's date of birth

13.4. Where permission is required for default judgment

C will require permission from the court to enter default judgment where:
  - ➢ C is seeking a non-money remedy
  - ➢ C is claiming for costs only
  - ➢ C is claiming against a child or protected party, or
    - ○ (A litigation friend must be appointed before default judgment entered)
  - ➢ C is claiming in tort against her civil partner

13.5. Applications to set aside default judgment: <u>CPR 13</u>

D may apply to set aside a default judgment entered against her.

Mandatory relief: <u>CPR 13.2</u>
The court **must** set aside default judgment when it has been wrongly entered. This will be where D has filed an AoS or Defence in time.

Discretionary relief: <u>CPR 13.3</u>
The court **may** set aside default judgment where:
  - ➢ D has a **real prospect** of successfully defending the claim, or
  - ➢ There is some other **good reason** why:

o Judgment should be set aside, or

o D should be allowed to defend

Any claim abandoned by C in order to secure default judgment will be restored if the judgment is set aside.

SUMMARY JUDGMENT: CPR 24

13.6. Requirements for summary judgment

Grounds

The grounds for summary judgment are that:[44]

- ➤ C has no real prospect of succeeding on the claim or issue, **or**
- ➤ D has no real prospect of successfully defending the claim or issue, **and**

- ➤ There is no other compelling reason why the case or issue should be disposed of at trial

Availability

Summary judgment is always available against C. It is not available against D in:

- ➤ Residential possession proceedings against a mortgagor or tenant, or
- ➤ An admiralty claim in rem

13.7. Summary judgment and counterclaims / set-off

Summary judgment is not available if there is some other compelling reason for a trial.

If the Respondent is counterclaiming or claims set-off then the Respondent may argue that the facts of the CC or set-off are so closely related to the claim that a trial is required.

---

[44] Note the similarity in this test to that of permission to appeal: see Chapter 26.1

The court has three possible options:

➤ It may accept R's argument and refuse to grant summary judgment,

➤ It may grant summary judgment but with a stay on enforcement pending trial of the CC, or

➤ If set-off is claimed, D must quantify the amount. The court may give summary judgment for the balance

Exception: the cheque rule

An exception to the general rule that a CC or set-off will avoid summary judgment is the cheque rule. If C applies for summary judgement after D's dishonoured cheque D will not be able to rely upon set-off. This rule has been extended to direct debit mandates.

13.8. Procedure for summary judgment

The application is made under Part 23. The applicant must identify any point of law or provision in a document that the applicant replies upon. The application should be supported by evidence.

The timeline for a summary judgment application is:

Step	Comment
[D files AoS / Defence]	[C may not apply until D has filed either an Acknowledgement of Service or Defence.]
A makes an application	R must have 14 days notice of the hearing date and the issues to be decided.
R files and serves evidence	R must file and serve evidence no less than 7 days before the hearing.

A files and serves evidence in reply	A must file and serve evidence in reply no less than 3 days before the hearing.
Hearing	The court will make one of the orders at Chapter 13.9 below.

13.9. Possible court orders

After hearing a summary judgment application the court will make / give one of four orders / judgments:

- ➤ Give (summary) judgment on the claim
- ➤ Strike out or dismiss the claim
- ➤ Dismiss the application
- ➤ Make a conditional order

The order the court makes will be accompanied by a costs order.

Conditional orders

Conditional orders are made when it is possible but improbable that a claim or Defence will succeed. Conditional orders are not final judgments. They require a party to:

- ➤ Pay a sum of money into court, or
- ➤ Take a specified step in relation to a claim or Defence

The court will strike out the claim or Defence in the event of non-compliance.

CHAPTER SUMMARY

- ➤ Summary judgment and default judgment are entirely distinct.
- ➤ Default judgment is sought where D has failed to file and serve a Defence.
- ➤ Summary judgment is sought where either party considers that there should be no trial at all.

14. CASE MANAGEMENT

The court has wide case management powers. The court routinely makes orders for procedural steps called 'directions' to assist case management.

14.1. Allocation between tracks and transfer: CPR 26

Allocation

The court will allocate every case to a track after the parties return the directions questionnaire. The scope of each track is shown in the table at Chapter 1.4.

The court has the power to subsequently re-allocate a case to a different track.

Automatic transfer

The court will automatically transfer certain types of claim. Designated money claims will be transferred to D's home court or preferred court. Non-designated money claims will be automatically transferred to D's home court where:

➤ The claim is for a specified sum, and
➤ D is an individual

14.2. Procedure at CMCs

A case management conference 'CMC' is used by the court to manage the progress of a case. It is usual for parties to make submissions on the directions required before the court makes the order. The court may make orders of its own initiative.[45]

---

[45] CPR 3.3

14.3. Typical directions on each track: <u>CPR 27 -29</u>

Typical directions on the small claims and fast track are as follows:

	Small claims	Fast Track
Disclosure	Each party to file and serve copies of all documents relied upon 14 days before hearing. Original documents brought to hearing.	Standard disclosure.
Witness statements	May be required, having regard to: ➤ The amount in dispute ➤ Whether the parties are represented ➤ Whether an order for further information would bring more clarity	Required. Service by simultaneous exchange.
Experts	No expert report without permission.	Joint expert (unless there is good reason). Usually no oral expert evidence.
Special directions	May order a party to clarify their case.	To confirm a trial date and provide for a trial bundle.

The multi-track is similar to the fast track. However:
- ➤ Standard disclosure is not the starting point in the multi-track (see Chapter 15.2)
- ➤ The court will be more willing to allow individual experts and oral expert evidence
- ➤ The court may consider a Pre-Trial Review necessary to settle a statement of issues to be tried and determine a timetable

Consent to directions

In both the fast and multi-track the parties may agree to vary the case management timetable as appropriate. Parties will not normally be able to change any fixed date of trial.

14.4. Costs and costs budgets

It is important to understand the different costs regimes that apply on different tracks.

Small claims: CPR 27.14

There is usually **no recovery of costs** in the small claims track. Recovery is limited to the costs of commencement and travel. Exceptionally, a party may recover their costs when the other party behaved unreasonably.

Fast track

Normal costs shifting applies. A fixed cost regime applies in RTAs, Employer Liability and Public Liability cases. The costs of the hearing are fixed.[46]

Multi-track: cost budgeting

Normal costs shifting applies. Except in the Commercial and Admiralty Courts a **cost budget** must be filed. The costs budget sets out how much each party expects to spend on each stage of the litigation.

The parties exchange budgets and, if they cannot agree, the court will fix the recoverable amount. When making a costs order the court will not depart from the costs budget unless there is a good reason.

The budget must be filed by the date specified in the notice of proposed allocation, or at the latest, 7 days before the first CMC. Failure to file a budget will mean that a party is limited to their court fees.

---

[46] CPR 45.38

CHAPTER SUMMARY

➤ The courts' wide case management powers are contained in CPR 3 and are informed by the overriding objective in CPR 1.1.

➤ Different directions will usually be given depending on the track.

➤ Costs budgeting applies to most cases in the multi-track.

15. DISCLOSURE AND INSPECTION OF DOCUMENTS

In many ways the topic of disclosure falls within case management powers of the court (see Chapter 14). Disclosure is formulaic and logical but requires memorizing many short lists.

Throughout this chapter 'A' is a party who may have a duty to disclose and permit inspection and 'B' is a party who may have a right to disclosure or inspection.

15.1. Disclosure and inspection: general

Definition: CPR 31.2 and 31.3
Disclosure and inspection is a **two-stage process**:
  (1) Disclosure: the parties exchange a list of all documents that support or adversely affect any party, as well as any documents over which privilege is claimed[47]
  (2) Inspection: the opponent has a right to inspect any non-privileged disclosed documents

B automatically acquires a right to inspect a document except where:
  ➢ The document is no longer under A's control
  ➢ A has a right or duty to withhold inspection (e.g. privilege), or
  ➢ A considers it disproportionate to the issues in the case to permit inspection

Timing
Following the case's allocation by the court to a track the court will give track-specific directions. It is at this stage that disclosure is usually ordered (see Chapter 14.3).

However, parties remain under a **continuing duty** to disclose documents that are brought to their notice until proceedings conclude.[48]

---

[47] For privilege, see Chapter 27.15 – 27.21
[48] CPR 31.11

Inadvertent disclosure: <u>CPR 31.20</u>

If a privileged document is accidentally released for inspection the inspecting party may use it **only** with the permission of the court.

15.2. Standard disclosure: <u>CPR 31.5 – 31.6</u>

'Standard disclosure' is the label for the level of disclosure normally expected by a court. It applies to all PI claims and all fast track claims.[49]

Once ordered as part of a court's directions, standard disclosure requires A to disclose documents that:
- ➢ A relies upon
- ➢ Adversely affect A's case
- ➢ Adversely affect another party's case, or
- ➢ Support another party's case

Procedure for standard disclosure: <u>CPR 31.10</u>
Standard disclosure requires:
- ➢ A lists the relevant documents
- ➢ The list must be in a convenient order and as concise as possible
- ➢ A list of the documents no longer in A's control and what happened to them, and
- ➢ A makes a 'Disclosure Statement' stating:
  - o The extent of the search
  - o That A understands its duty to disclose
  - o That A has carried out that duty

Duty of search: <u>CPR 31.7</u>
A is required to conduct a reasonable search. Reasonableness is determined by reference to:
- ➢ The number of documents
- ➢ The nature and complexity of proceedings
- ➢ The ease and expense of document retrieval, and
- ➢ The significance of a document

---

[49] There is no disclosure on the small claims track: see Chapter 14

Definition of control: CPR 31.8

A document is deemed to be under A's control where A:

> ➤ Is or was in physical possession of it
> ➤ Has or had the right to possession of it, or
> ➤ Has or had the right to inspect and take copies of it

15.3. Disclosure in non-PI multi-track cases: CPR 31.5(3) – (8)

Different rules apply in a non-PI multi-track case. They are designed to encourage the parties to agree disclosure and / or to allow the court to direct disclosure appropriate to the case.

A joint pre-disclosure report must be filed and served not less than 14 days before the first CMC. The parties must meet to attempt to agree a disclosure proposal not less than 7 days before the first CMC.

The Court retains wide-ranging powers to make numerous disclosure orders, including on an issue-by-issue basis. The emphasis is on flexibility.

15.4. Specific disclosure: CPR 31.12

Where B believes that disclosure has been inadequate B can apply for an order for specific disclosure.

An order for 'specific disclosure' requires that A must:

> ➤ Disclose the documents specified in the order,
> ➤ Carry out a search to the extent stated in the order, and
> ➤ Disclose any documents located as a result of that search

An order for 'specific inspection' requires that despite A considering that it would be disproportionate to allow inspection, A must nevertheless allow inspection.

Applications for orders for specific disclosure or inspection are made under CPR 23 using an application notice (see Chapter 12.2).

15.5. Collateral use of disclosed documents: CPR 31.22

The general rule is that B may use a document disclosed by an opponent for the purpose of those proceedings only **unless**:
> The document in question has been read to or by the court in public
> The court gives permission, or
> The parties agree on its collateral use

15.6. *Norwich Pharmacal*[50] orders: CPR 31.8

Where the identity of a wrongdoer is unknown to the party seeking to bring a claim, any TP is under a duty to assist that party by providing full information and disclosing the identity of the wrongdoer. An order can be sought to ensure that a TP fulfils that duty. Such an order can only be sought if:
> The information cannot be obtained by other means, and
> The wronged party has a real interest in suing the wrongdoer

The order is sought by making an interim application to a QBD Master or ChD judge, supported by evidence.

15.7. Pre-action disclosure: CPR 31.16

A prospective party to any proceedings may apply to the court for disclosure of documents using a <u>Part 23</u> application notice. The rules do not support blind 'fishing expeditions'.

Conditions for pre-action disclosure:
> The respondent is likely to be a party to subsequent proceedings, and
> The applicant is likely to be a party to those proceedings, and
> Hypothetically, standard disclosure would apply to the document the applicant is seeking, and
> Disclosure before issue of proceedings is desirable to:
>> o Dispose fairly of anticipated proceedings, or

---

[50] [1974] AC 133

- o   Assist the dispute to be resolved without proceedings, or
- o   Save costs

In assessing whether ordering pre-action disclosure is 'desirable' a court undertakes a two-stage process: the jurisdictional and discretionary stages.[51] The former stage addresses whether there is a real prospect of such an order being fair to the parties and the latter is based on the court's assessment of all the facts.

The costs of pre-action disclosure are considered as a special case under CPR 46.1. The general rule is that the person against whom the order is sought will pay the opposition's costs of making the application and of complying with the order.

15.8. Non-party disclosure: CPR 31.17

The court has the power to order disclosure against a non-party to proceedings following a Part 23 application notice or on its own initiative. As with pre-action disclosure, these rules do not support blind 'fishing expeditions'.

Conditions for non-party disclosure:
Once proceedings have started, the court **may** order non-party disclosure where:
- ➢ The document is likely to support the applicant or adversely affect another party, and
- ➢ Disclosure is necessary to dispose fairly of the claim or to save costs

CHAPTER SUMMARY
- ➢ Disclosure and inspection is a two-stage process.
- ➢ The standard disclosure rules are not used for non-PI, multi-track cases.
- ➢ Parties are under a continuing duty of disclosure.

---

[51] *Black v Sumitomo Corporation* [2001] EWCA Civ 1819

16. Sanctions, Strike Out, Stays and Discontinuance

The court's general case management powers (see Chapter 14) extend to issuing sanctions against parties, staying claims and even striking out statements of case. Cs may also halt their own cases by discontinuing proceedings.

16.1. Sanctions

The court uses sanctions to ensure compliance with rules and orders. The court may impose a sanction at any hearing, either after application or of its own motion. The court will not usually allow a failure to comply with directions to postpone a trial unless the circumstances are exceptional.

The likely sanction for **minor breaches** is that:
> ➤ The court will allow the party in breach limited time to comply, and / or
> ➤ The court will make a costs order against the party in breach

The likely sanction for **serious breaches** is that:
> ➤ Any revised deadline set by the court will be final, although a very serious breach may result in the immediate imposition of a sanction
> ➤ The court will make a costs order against the party in breach, and / or
> ➤ The court may make an unless order

Unless orders
An 'unless order' states that unless a party complies with a **specific step** in a **specific time** proceedings a sanction (usually the striking out of a Particulars of Claim or Defence) will apply. The court will only make an unless order if it is satisfied that a sanction is appropriate. The party in breach should appeal the unless order, as opposed to seeking relief from sanctions. Refer to Chapter 23.6.

Relief from sanctions: CPR 3.9

Parties may apply to the court to grant relief from sanctions. In granting relief, the court will consider all the circumstances of the case so as to deal justly with the application, including the need:

> For litigation to be conducted efficiently and at proportionate cost, and
> To enforce compliance with rules / PDs / court orders

The last consideration was added following the **Jackson reforms** and has led to a stricter approach.

16.2. Strike out: CPR 3.4

Striking out a statement of case means that it is deleted and can no longer be relied upon. If a Particulars of Claim is struck out that is the end of C's claim.[52] If a Defence is struck out C will be entitled to default judgment (see Chapter 13). If default judgment has been entered against a D after her Defence was struck out D may apply under CPR 3.6 for relief.

The test

A statement of case will be struck out if:

> There are **no reasonable grounds** for bringing or defending a claim (e.g a bare denial)
> The proceedings are an abuse of the court's process, or
> There has been a failure to comply with a rule / PD / court order

Discretion

The court has a discretion when considering striking out. The court may:

> Allow a party to amend their statement of case, or
> Treat the application as one for summary judgment (see Chapter 13)

---

[52] A new claim must not be res judicata: see Chapter 27.3

16.3. Procedure for sanctions or strike out

Procedure

An application for sanctions or for strike out is an interim application made under CPR 23 (see Chapter 12.2). It is usually made with notice.

No evidence is needed for a strike out application. Despite this, evidence is usually filed and served.

Following the application there will be a hearing. If strike out is sought on the basis that there are no reasonable grounds for bringing or defending the claim then the hearing will assume that the facts stated in the statement of case are true.

Timing

Applications for sanctions should be made as early as possible. Applications for strike out should be made as soon as it is obvious that they should be made. This will usually be between the acknowledgment of service and the directions questionnaire.

16.4. Stays: s 49 Senior Courts Act 1981

A stay is a halting of proceedings. No step may be taken in the proceedings aside from applying to lift the stay.

The court will routinely order a stay where:
- ➤ A Part 36 offer has been accepted (see Chapter 20)
- ➤ There has been a *Tomlin* order (see Chapter 23.5)
- ➤ C has a pending medical examination, or
- ➤ C has failed to pay D's costs after discontinuing part of a claim

Stays pending medical examination

Cs in PI cases will routinely be required to undergo medical examination. A claim will be stayed where:
- ➤ D admits liability but there is a lack of evidence as a clear prognosis is not yet available

- A claim has been issued close to the end of limitation but there is not sufficient evidence, or
- C unreasonably refuses to undergo medical examination

16.5. Discontinuance: CPR 38

General rule: no permission needed
The general rule is that parties may discontinue all or part of a claim at any time against any number of Ds.

When permission is required
Permission is required to discontinue in the following circumstances:
- Where there has been an interim injunction[53]
- Where there has been an undertaking in damages[54]
- Where there has been an interim payment[55]
  - (Instead of court permission C can seek permission in writing from D)
- Where there is more than one C, or
  - (Instead of court permission C can seek permission in writing from all other Cs)
- Where C is under a disability[56]

Procedure for discontinuance
In order to discontinue C must:
- File a notice of discontinuance, and
- Serve a copy on all parties

A D who has not consented to discontinuance may apply to set aside the discontinuance. D's application must be made within 28 days after receiving the notice of discontinuance.

---

[53] See Chapter 18
[54] See Chapter 18.4
[55] See Chapter 17
[56] See Chapters 3.6 and 4.6

Cost consequences of discontinuing

The general rule is that the discontinuing party pays all the costs of all the parties up until the date of service of discontinuance. The costs are limited to the part of the claim that was discontinued.

There are two exceptions to the general rule:
- ➤ If the claim was proceeding in the small claims track, or
- ➤ If C has, in effect, obtained the relief C was seeking in the claim

Costs will usually be payable at the end of the claim but can be payable immediately. If C fails to pay the court will impose a stay on the remaining proceedings.

CHAPTER SUMMARY
- ➤ The test for strike out is different to that for summary judgment.
- ➤ Discontinuance is a voluntary choice by C to no longer pursue a claim. By contrast, sanctions, strike out and stays are orders of the court.
- ➤ Parties may seek relief from sanctions under CPR 3.9. The test has been changed following the Jackson reforms.

17. INTERIM PAYMENTS AND SECURITY FOR COSTS

These two types of interim order appear at first glance similar. However, they are sought for different reasons by different parties.

Interim payments are sought by C against D. Security for costs is usually sought by D against C (unless there is a CC).

INTERIM PAYMENTS

An interim payment is defined as an order for payment of a sum of money by D on account of any damages, debt, or other sum (except costs) which the court may hold D liable to pay.[57]

17.1. The principles and procedure relating to applications for interim payments

Principles
Orders for interim payments may be sought where C considers that she is likely to achieve some success in the claim and that it would be unjust to delay payment of that money until after trial.

The underlying rationale of an interim payment is to support a C who has suffered a loss and might otherwise have to wait for long periods of time before receiving damages to compensate them.

An order for an interim payment is not wholly disadvantageous to D since D's liability to pay interest on the total award will be reduced.

If an order for an interim payment is made following an interim application, C must be careful not to disclose this to the trial judge until all questions of liability and quantum have been determined (unless D consents).[58] This is fair because otherwise an indication of another

---

[57] CPR 25.1(1)(k)
[58] CPR 25.9

judge's ruling on the likelihood of C's success in the case may influence the trial judge's opinion.

Procedure: CPR 25.6(1)

An application for an interim payment order cannot be made until the period for filing an Acknowledgment of Service has expired. Applications are made on notice to D and must be served at least 14 clear days before the hearing of the application. They must also be supported by evidence served with the application.

Evidence: PD25B [2.1]

The supporting evidence should set out all relevant matters including:
- The amount sought
- What the money will be used for
- The likely amount of the total award
- The reasons for believing the relevant ground is satisfied
- In a PI claim, details of special damages and past and future loss, and
- In a claim under Fatal Accidents Act 1976, details of the persons on whose behalf the claim is made and the nature of the claim

17.2. Grounds for applying for interim payments: CPR 25.7

An interim payment may be only be ordered if:
- D has admitted liability to pay C
- C has obtained judgment against D
- The court is satisfied that, if the claim went to trial, C would obtain judgment against D for a substantial amount of money
- C is seeking possession of land, and the court is satisfied that if the case went to trial D would be held liable to pay C a sum of money for use and occupation of the land, **or**
- The claim is brought against more than one D, and the further conditions are satisfied

The grounds set out in CPR 25.7 are the only grounds under which an interim payment can be ordered.

Cases with more than one D: CPR 25.7(1)(e)

A court may make an interim payment order where:

> ➤ There are 2 or more Ds
> ➤ The court is satisfied that if the claim went to trial C would obtain judgment for a substantial sum of money (other than costs) against at least one of D
> ➤ The court cannot determine which D will lose, and
> ➤ All of the defendants are either insured, public bodies, or are Ds whose liability will be met by an insurer[59]

The effect of set-offs and CCs: CPR 25.7(5)

The court must take into account any relevant set-off or CC and any contributory negligence.

CCs affect the likely **amount** of the final award. Therefore, once the principle of an interim order being granted has been decided by a court, the court will move on to consider the amount as a second stage. If D's CC is worth more than the claim itself an interim payment may not be appropriate.

Set-offs are also defences. Therefore, in contrast to CCs, the existence of a set-off goes to the first stage of the court's decision on an interim payment order: the **grounds** for granting the order. If the set-off defence has a reasonable prospect of success the court may not be satisfied that C would obtain judgment against D.

17.3. The amount to be ordered by way of interim payment: CPR 25.7(4) - (5)

The court is not permitted to order an interim payment of more than a **reasonable proportion** of the likely amount of any final judgment, taking into account any contributory negligence and any relevant set-off or CC.

Therefore, the court must take the structured approach of:

> ➤ Calculating the likely final award

---

[59] s 151 Road Traffic Act 1988

> Discounting the probability / value of any CC / set-off / CN, and
> Reducing the amount again to arrive at a reasonable proportion

SECURITY FOR COSTS

The question of who pays costs is not usually addressed until the merits of the claim have been determined. However, in order to protect Ds facing an expensive defence of potentially unjustified claims D can seek security for costs in limited circumstances.

17.4. Procedure on applications for security for costs

Principles

Where a significant risk exists that D has no real prospect of recovering her costs if she is ultimately successful D can apply to the court for an order for security for costs.

Unlike interim payments orders for security for costs are made against parties in the position of C. This means that the order may be sought by D in a standard claim or by C where D has counterclaimed. In this chapter the party seeking the order will be referred to as D and the party against whom it is sought referred to as C.

The test: <u>CPR 25.13</u>
To make an order for security for costs, the court must be satisfied that:
1. One of the conditions in <u>CPR 25.13(2)</u> is satisfied
2. Having regard to all the circumstances of the case, it would be just to exercise the court's discretion in favour of making the order, **and**
3. The amount of security is sufficient

Procedure
The effect of an order for security for costs is to require C to pay a sum of money into court. This acts as security if C's claim is unsuccessful and D is awarded her costs. Until the payment is made into court, C's

claim is stayed.

An application for security for costs is normally made by D with notice at the first CMC using the standard CPR 23 procedure. It should be accompanied by written evidence.

C should be served with the application notice at least 3 clear days before the hearing of the application.[60]

17.5. Specific conditions: CPR 25.13(2)

One of the six conditions in CPR 25.13(2) must be satisfied.[61]

C is resident outside the jurisdiction: CPR 25.13(2)(a)

In order for this condition to be satisfied C must be resident out of the jurisdiction (England and Wales) but not resident in a European Member-State.

Residence is determined by C's 'habitual or normal residence' and is a question of fact and degree.[62] D carries the burden of proof.

The underlying rationale of this condition is that C's ability to pay D's costs is of greatest concern where C has foreign assets.

C is an insolvent company: CPR 25.13(2)(c)

In order for this condition to be satisfied C must be a company and there must be reason to believe C will be unable to pay D's costs if ordered.

Evidence to indicate that C will be unable to pay any of D's costs include proof that C is in insolvency proceedings or signed witness statements of C's inability to pay.

---

[60] CPR 23.7(1)(b)
[61] The syllabus only refers to two of the six conditions
[62] *Lysaght v IRC* [1928] AC 234

17.6. Exercise of discretion to order security for costs: CPR 25.13(1)(a) and 25.14(1)(a)

Once it has been established that the case comes within one of the conditions set out in CPR 25.13(2) the court must consider whether it is just to make the order.

In determining whether it is just to make the order, a court will have regard to all the circumstances, including:
> The merits of the claim (without the court conducting a mini-trial)
> The impact on C of being required to give security
> Delay by D in making an application
> Whether C's limited financial means has been caused by D, **and**
> D's other options to recover costs

If the court elects to exercise its discretion in favour of D, the final stage is to establish an appropriate amount for the security payment by C.

17.7. Power to make orders subject to conditions: CPR 3.1(3)

Using its extensive case management powers under CPR 3.1, the court retains the power to make an order subject to conditions.

For example, before granting an interim order, the court may require the party seeking it to provide an undertaking in case the party whom it is against suffers loss. Alternatively, the court could require the parties to meet a particular deadline for service and filing of documents or evidence.

CHAPTER SUMMARY
> Interim payments and security for costs may both be granted as interim orders by a court but serve very different purposes.
> Security for costs can only be ordered against a party bringing a claim.

18. INTERIM INJUNCTIONS

Injunctions can be sought as a final remedy (see Chapters 7 and 8). The courts have also recognised the need to grant injunctions on an 'interim' basis. Such an interim injunction lasts until trial when the court will either grant a final injunction or discharge the interim injunction.

In this chapter 'A' is an Applicant applying for an interim injunction and 'R' is a Respondent challenging that interim injunction.

18.1. Procedure for interim injunctions

An application for an interim injunction is made with an application notice. The application notice must state:
> What order A is seeking, and
> The date, time and place of the hearing

The application notice should usually be served on R. If A makes a without notice application there must be good reasons for not giving notice.[63] A without notice application should contain a **'return date'** (see Chapter 12.1).

Evidence: PD 25A [3]
The application notice must include evidence in a W/S or statement of case setting out:
> The facts upon which A relies, **and**
> All material facts of which the court should be made aware

Timing
The application may be made at any time. It should be made as soon as it becomes apparent that it is necessary. D may not apply for an interim injunction unless D has filed an AoS or Defence.

---

[63] CPR 25.3

If an application is made with notice, it should be made not less than **3 clear days** before the application will be dealt with. If there is not sufficient time to give notice, informal notice should be given.

18.2. *American Cyanamid* principles

When determining whether to grant an interim injunction the court will follow the principles set out in the *American Cyanamid* case.[64]

The court will ask:
- ➤ Whether there is a **serious issue** to be tried,
- ➤ If so, **whether damages would be an adequate remedy** for a party injured by the grant of, or the failure to grant, an interim injunction, and
- ➤ If damages would not be adequate for either party, the court will look to the **balance of convenience**

Serious issue to be tried
It is usually reasonably easy to meet the requirement for a 'serious issue to be tried'. It will usually be met if A can show an arguable cause of action on the facts that A asserts. It does not mean that A must be able to show that A is more likely than not to win. Where R has no defence to the claim then there is no serious issue, but instead A will be entitled to the injunction.

Adequacy of damages
If A could be adequately compensated in damages for the loss A is suffering and will continue to suffer without the injunction then no injunction will be granted. There is simply no need – A will compensated with damages after trial.

Likewise, if R could be adequately compensated in damages for the loss R will suffer as a result of the injunction, then the injunction will be granted.

---

[64] *American Cyanamid Co v Ethicon Ltd* [1975] AC 396

Cases in which parties will argue that they cannot be adequately compensated by damages will involve cases where losses are difficult to quantify. It may be hard to say whether R's launch of a new product (which A says breaches A's intellectual property) would have been a profitable success or a failure, or something in between.

Balance of convenience
If neither A nor R would be adequately compensated with damages then the court will look to the balance of convenience. This will involve:

> ➤ Preserving the '*status quo ante*' (i.e. the position as it was)
> ➤ Avoiding the risk of injustice, and
> ➤ Looking at the relative strength of each parties' case

This is a difficult test to apply. It can be difficult to work out what the 'status quo' that should be preserved is. The courts are reluctant to have recourse to the relative strength of each parties' case.

18.3. Exceptions to *American Cyanamid*

There are a number of exceptions to the *American Cyanamid* principles.

Mandatory interim injunctions
In an application for a mandatory interim injunction (requiring R to do an act) the court will require a high probability that the substantive claim will succeed.

Where the interim injunction will finally dispose of the case
If an interim injunction would finally dispose of the case the court should consider the degree of likelihood that A will succeed at trial. A higher likelihood will mean the injunction is more likely to be granted. An example of a case where an interim injunction would finally dispose of the case would be where the alleged infringement is short lived and will expire before trial, such as a two-week building project that is allegedly a nuisance.

Where the injunction would restrict freedom of expression

If the injunction would restrict R's freedom of expression then different principles apply. The <u>Human Rights Act 1998</u> requires that A is 'likely' to win at trial. The courts have emphasised that this is a flexible test. While 'likely' does not mean 'more likely than not' it is clear that this is a higher threshold than merely showing a serious issue to be tried.

Where A's application for an injunction is to prevent freedom of expression but also asserts a right to privacy then the court must weigh the two competing rights. The law is outside the scope of this book.

18.4. Undertakings and cross-undertakings

A cross-undertaking in damages is a promise to the court to pay any loss suffered by the opposition as a result of the injunction. Generally A will be required to give a cross-undertaking to compensate any loss suffered by R as a result of the injunction. R 'undertakes' to abide by the injunction and A 'cross-undertakes' to compensate R for any loss. If A does not give the undertaking no injunction will be granted.

The court may further consider whether to require an undertaking from A to pay TPs to the claim.

CHAPTER SUMMARY

➢ An interim injunction is not available if damages would be an adequate remedy.

➢ In order to have an interim injunction ordered A must be prepared to make a cross-undertaking.

➢ When one of the exceptions to *American Cyanamid* applies the normal test is either not applicable or is altered.

20. OFFERS TO SETTLE

Parties may settle proceedings at any point. A special type of offer, called a Part 36 offer, is designed to encourage settlement. Part 36 offers have important cost consequences and, as a result, a well-timed Part 36 offer can put much pressure on the opposition. In order to gain the benefits of a Part 36 offer the requirements of CPR 36 must be met.

CPR 36 does not apply to the small claims track.[65]

20.1. Requirements for a Part 36 offer

Making a Part 36 offer: CPR 36.7(1)
A Part 36 offer is made when it is **served** on the offeree. One of the prescribed methods of service should be used.[66]

Formalities: CPR 36.2(2)
A Part 36 offer **must**:
  ➢ Be made in writing (either by letter or court form)
  ➢ Clearly state that it is intended to have the consequences of CPR 36
  ➢ Specify a period of not less than 21 days within which D will be liable for C's costs if the offer is accepted
  ➢ State whether it relates to the whole or part of the claim, **and**
  ➢ State whether it takes into account any CC

Terms of a Part 36 offer
The terms of a Part 36 offer need to:
  ➢ Be sufficiently certain for an effective contract to be formed if the offer is accepted
  ➢ Clearly indicate whether the offer is in full and final settlement, and
  ➢ Offer a single sum of money (for money claims)

---

[65] CPR 27.2(1)(g)
[66] CPR 6.20 (see Chapter 4.4)

Additional requirements for PI claims

For a PI claim the Part 36 offer must additionally:

> Comply with requirements relating to recovery of State benefits, and

> Address further requirements if the claim includes future pecuniary loss or seeks provisional damages

Failure to comply with the formalities

A significant departure from the formalities of CPR 36.2(2) will mean that an offer will not qualify as a Part 36 offer. By contrast, minor procedural defects in Part 36 offers may still be corrected by applying to the court to exercise its discretionary case management powers under CPR 3.10.

20.2. The relevant period: CPR 36.3(1)

A Part 36 offer must specify a 'relevant period'. If the offer is accepted within the relevant period then D will be liable for C's costs.[67]

Minimum relevant periods

If a Part 36 offer is made more than 21 days before trial the relevant period must be **greater than or equal to 21 days**. If a Part 36 offer is made less than 21 days before trial, the relevant period is the period up to the end of the trial or such other period as the court may determine.

20.3. Consequences of accepting Part 36 offers

Acceptance during the relevant period

A Part 36 offer is accepted through the offeree serving a written notice of acceptance on the offeror and filing it with the court.

The usual consequence of the offeree's acceptance is that:

> D must pay **C's standard basis costs** (see Chapter 22.6) up to the date of notice of acceptance[68]

> The claim is **stayed: CPR 36.11(1)**, and

---

[67] CPR 36.10
[68] There is an exception for low value RTA claims: Section II, CPR 45

> Payment must be made within 14 days: CPR 36.11(6)

Acceptance after the relevant period has expired
A Part 36 offer may be accepted at any time so long as it has not been withdrawn.

Where a Part 36 offer is accepted after the relevant period the parties may agree the liability for costs. If they do not, the court will usually order that:
> C is entitled to costs up to the expiry of the relevant period, and
> The offeree will be liable for the offeror's costs for the period from the expiry of the relevant period to the date of acceptance, and
> Costs are assessed on the standard basis

The court retains the discretion to make a different costs order.

Acceptance relating to part of the claim: CPR 36.10(2)
A Part 36 offer may be made in respect of only a part of a claim. Acceptance of a Part 36 offer relating to only part of the claim results in an end to proceedings only if C abandons the remaining 'live' part of the claim.

If the 'live' part is not abandoned, the parties proceed to trial, and the court then has a discretion regarding the costs of the 'dead' part of the claim.

20.4. Withdrawing, reducing and increasing offers to settle

Before the expiry of the relevant period: CPR 36.3(5)
Before the expiry of the relevant period a Part 36 offer may be withdrawn or its terms changed only with the court's permission.

After the expiry of the relevant period
After the expiry of the relevant period a Part 36 offer that has not been accepted can be withdrawn. The offeror's withdrawal or change of terms is simply done by serving written notice on the offeree.

The effect of a withdrawn Part 36 offer: CPR 36.14(6)(a)

A withdrawn Part 36 offer no longer carries with it the costs and interest consequences that flow under CPR 36. It can still be relevant to assessing the parties' willingness to settle if made 'without prejudice save as to costs' (see Chapter 22.8).

20.5. Consequences of failing to beat a Part 36 offer: CPR 36.14(1) – (6)

When an offeree rejects a Part 36 offer to settle she should be aware of the potential consequences. Indeed, an offeror may use the consequences set out at CPR 36.14 to apply tactical pressure to the offeree.

There are consequences where:
> ➤ C fails to obtain a judgment more advantageous than D's Part 36 offer, (C fails to beat D's offer) or
> ➤ Judgment against D is at least as advantageous to C as the C's Part 36 offer (D fails to beat C's offer)

C fails to beat D's Part 36 offer: CPR 36.14(2)
Unless the court considers it unjust to do so, C will pay D:
(a) D's costs from the expiry of the relevant period expired, and
(b) Interest on those costs (not more than 10% above the base rate)

D fails to beat C's Part 36 offer: CPR 36.14(3)
Unless the court considers it unjust to do so, D will pay C:
(a) Interest on the judgment (not more than 10% above base rate) from the expiry of the relevant period
(b) C's costs on an **indemnity** basis
(c) Interest on those costs (not more than 10% above the base rate), and
(d) An additional amount

The additional amount is 10% of the first £500,000 awarded and 5% of any amount awarded after the first £500,000. It cannot exceed £75,000.

C deserves the extra consequences because if C wins at trial C will normally be entitled to costs on the standard basis (see Chapter 22.6). To further encourage C's to make Part 36 offers the **Jackson reforms** proposed the additional amount.

Definition of 'unjust': CPR 36.14(4)

In determining whether it would be unjust to make a costs order after a party failed to beat a Part 36 offer, the court will take into account **all the circumstances** of the case including:

> - The terms of any Part 36 offer
> - The stage in proceedings when the Part 36 was made
> - The information available at the time when the Part 36 offer was made, and
> - The conduct of the parties with regard to the giving or refusing to give information to enable an offer to be evaluated

20.6. Secrecy relating to offers to settle, and the consequences of breach

Non-disclosure to the judge: CPR 36.13(2)

The fact there has been a Part 36 offer must **not** be disclosed to the court at trial until all questions of liability and remedies have been decided. If all the parties agree in writing, the offer can be disclosed.[69]

The general rule applies to trials and not interim applications. This is because the eventual trial judge will not hear the interim applications.

Consequences of breach of secrecy

If the fact there has been a Part 36 offer is disclosed in error to the trial judge the trial judge has a discretion whether to continue with the trial or to withdraw.

If the trial judge does withdraw the responsible party is likely to bear the costs of the wasted trial.

---

[69] CPR 36.13(3)(c)

CHAPTER SUMMARY

- Merely because the offeror fails to comply with the requirements of <u>CPR 36</u> does not make the offer to settle invalid. The offer survives. It simply does not have the normal consequences of a Part 36 offer.

- Both C and D can make Part 36 offers. C stands to gain more than D if D fails to beat C's offer because absent any offer C will normally be entitled to standard costs.

21. TRIAL

The trial is the culmination of the steps taken by the parties in the case. The judge will hear the evidence and decide the issues.

21.1. Witness summonses: CPR 34.2 – 34.7

A witness summons may be used to achieve two different objectives. It can compel the named witness to:
- ➤ Give oral evidence at trial, and / or
- ➤ Produce specified documents at trial

If a party seeks to compel a witness ('W') to give evidence or produce documents the issue of a witness summons is purely a formality. Once the fee is paid and the relevant practice form completed and sealed by the court the witness summons takes effect.

If W fails to comply with a witness summons in the county court W may be fined. In the High Court such a failure can be punished as contempt of court.

CPR 34.2(4)(b) provides that a witness summons may require W to produce documents to the court. The court may require earlier production to enable the parties sight of the documents prior to the hearing.

Under CPR 34.5(1), the general rule is that a witness summons will only bind W if it is served at least 7 days before the hearing date.

21.2. Skeleton arguments

A skeleton argument is a concise summary of the background facts and core submissions of each party. It is prepared for use by the judge at trial. It is designed to clarify issues and assist the judge in sorting through the bundle(s) of evidence and precedents. It should contain references to the bundle(s).

Skeleton arguments are not compulsory in the county courts but are often used. The specialist practice guides encourage the use of skeleton arguments in the High Court in hearings before a judge.

The Chancery Guide (applicable to the ChD) recommends the general use of skeleton arguments.[70]

The Queen's Bench Guide (applicable to the QBD generally) recommends the use of skeleton arguments for trials and substantial applications. Skeleton arguments should be filed and served not less than 2 days before trial. Chronologies are encouraged.[71]

The Admiralty and Commercial Courts Guide (applicable to the Admiralty and Commercial Courts within the QBD), although in favour of skeleton arguments, specifically encourages brevity. The Guide makes it clear that skeleton arguments are not a substitute for oral argument.[72]

In JR proceedings the applicant is required to file and serve a skeleton argument not less than 21 working days before the hearing with a bundle.[73]

See Chapter 26.7 for skeleton arguments in appeals.

21.3. Procedure on a civil trial

The CPR, PDs and specialist court practice guides provide courts with a general framework of how a civil trial may be conducted. Subject to that basic framework, the courts retain a wide discretion as to how to proceed.

Trial timetables

Trial timetables provide the structure within which counsel for all

---

[70] Exceptions exist where the application does not warrant one and where urgency requires: 1A-69, Chancery Guide
[71] 1B-51, Queen's Bench Guide
[72] 2A-29, Admiralty and Commercial Courts Guide
[73] CPR 54.16.4

parties must operate. They provide estimates as to how long the judge expects each element of the trial to take.

On the fast track, following the completion of the pre-trial checklist, the court will give any directions for the trial it considers appropriate, including a trial timetable.[74] CPR 28.6.5 provides a specimen trial timetable which acts as a template for fast track trials. The maximum of 5 hours presumes the trial judge has pre-read the papers.

On the multi-track, following the filing of a pre-trial checklist or the holding of a pre-trial review, the court will set a timetable for the trial.[75] The parties will then be notified of the trial timetable and the date for trial will be confirmed.

Timeline of a civil trial
A civil trial will normally be heard in the following order:
> C's opening speech
> D's opening speech
> XX of C's witnesses by D
> RX by C
> XX of D's witnesses by C
> RX by D
> D's submissions
> C's submissions
> Judgment
> Costs and consequential orders

Calling and examining witnesses: CPR 32.2 – 32.13
The usual method by which the evidence of Ws is produced at trial is by calling the W. The traditional approach in civil trials is that following the service of a witness statement the witness is called. Having been sworn in or affirmed, they verify the statement is theirs. The W/S then stands as that W's XIC unless the court orders otherwise.[76] The party not calling W will then have an opportunity to XX that

---

[74] CPR 28.6(1)(b)
[75] Unless one has already been fixed or the court considers it inappropriate: CPR 29.8(c)(i)
[76] CPR 32.5(2)

witness using leading questions. That W can be RX on the matters raised in XX using non-leading questions.

21.4. Judgment, Costs and Appeal

Judgment

Following the presentation of evidence and submissions from both parties the judge will be in a position to review the arguments made and reach a decision.

When the judge gives the judgment will depend on the complexity of the case and the judge's own professional commitments. In a straightforward trial judgment may be given immediately. In more complicated commercial matters judgment will often be reserved.

Once judgment is pronounced, it must be drawn up. See Chapter 23 (Judgments and Orders).

Submissions on orders for costs

After judgment has been entered the question of costs remains. If the CPR and PDs allow it, costs will be summarily assessed based on submission from both parties immediately after judgment. If the CPR or PDs prevent this, costs will be determined at a detailed assessment at a later date.

If costs are summarily assessed, counsel for both parties will make submissions on the appropriate costs order the court should make. Counsel should draw the judge's attention to all the circumstances of the case. See Chapter 22 (Costs, Funding and Civil Legal Aid).

Permission to appeal

An unsuccessful party at trial may orally apply at the end of the hearing for permission to appeal the judgment just pronounced.[77] If the court refuses permission to appeal, the unsuccessful party may elect to make a further application for permission to appeal to an appeal court.
The test for granting permission to appeal is found at <u>CPR 52.3(6)</u> and

---

[77] <u>CPR 52.3(2)</u>

is addressed in more detail at Chapter 26 (Appeals).

CHAPTER SUMMARY

> The civil approach to witness handling differs from the criminal approach. The W/S will usually stand as a W's XIC (subject to permission to amplify).

> Skeleton arguments are crucial to complex cases. Boiling the multiple bundles down to the core issues assists the judge and promotes a more efficient use of the court's time and resources.

22. Costs

'The subject of costs, which would deserve only modest attention in a well-balanced system, requires extensive treatment in England'.[78]

22.1. The difference between funding and costs orders

Funding is concerned with providing the finance to run a claim or defence (or other legal proceedings). The different types of funding are set out below.

By contrast costs orders are judge-made instructions as to whether a party should pay for the opposition's costs. Costs orders may be made after any interim hearing, the trial, or any other appeal / enforcement hearing.

Two central principles are used to determine costs orders:
- Costs payable by a party are at the discretion of the court. That includes:
    - Whether they are payable at all
    - If they are, the amount of those costs
- Costs **'follow the event'**. This means that the unsuccessful party pays the successful party's costs. However, this general rule is also subject to the court's discretion[79]

22.2. Types of private funding

Self-Funding
The simplest method of funding litigation is for a party to pay for it themselves. The expense and risk of this method explains the number of different funding options below.

---

[78] A Zuckerman, Principles of Civil Procedure, (2nd edn, Sweet & Maxwell 2006) 999
[79] CPR 44.2(4) – (5)

Before The Event Insurance ('BTE')

A party may take out insurance to cover them for legal costs in future legal disputes. For individuals, BTE is typically found as part of home or vehicle insurance policies.

After The Event Insurance ('ATE')

By contrast, even after the beginning of a legal dispute, a party can approach an insurer and negotiate the taking out of insurance to cover legal costs. Usually what is covered is only the risk of paying the opponent's costs.

Unless the prospects of success are high, ATE is very expensive. The premium charged by the insurer accounts for the predicted level of the opponent's costs and the probability of losing.

ATE premiums are generally no longer recoverable as part of a party's costs.[80]

Third party / Litigation funding

The funder and the party enter into a contractual agreement in which the funder agrees to finance all or part of the party's litigation costs. In return, the funder takes a share of the award if the party succeeds.

A fine line exists between litigation funding (which is lawful and increasingly popular) and champerty (which is contrary to public policy and still considered unlawful).[81] The key difference is that a litigation funder must not control the litigation.

Conditional Fee Agreement ('CFA')

This is often labelled as a: 'no win, no fee' agreement. If the party succeeds, the legal representative is entitled to its costs plus an uplift, or success fee (a percentage of the base costs).

---

[80] s 46(2) LASPO 2012. There is an exception for expert reports on liability and causation in clinical negligence disputes

[81] Champerty is based on maintenance. Maintenance is traditionally defined as the (financial) supporting or intermeddling in litigation without just cause. Champerty is considered an aggravated form of maintenance where the person intermeddling seeks to obtain a share in the expected award

Following the **Jackson reforms** the success fee is no longer recoverable from the opposition.[82]

22.3. Private funding – QOCS: CPR 44.13 – 44.16

Under QOCS, if C loses, C will not have to pay D's costs. By contrast, if C wins, D remains liable to pay C's costs. Therefore, costs can only 'shift one way' (to D, but not to C).

QOCS was introduced following the **Jackson reforms** to protect Cs who, as a matter of social policy, were deemed worth protecting from adverse costs. Its introduction was designed to counter-balance the abolition of success fees for CFAs and the recoverability of ATE premiums.

QOCS is **only available** to Cs in claims for **damages for PI** or under the Fatal Accidents Act 1976.

Qualifications

The general one-way costs shifting rule is not absolute, but 'qualified'. Two exceptions exist to prevent C from abusing the QOCS general rule.

First qualification – proceedings struck out

Under CPR 44.15, orders for costs against C may be fully enforced **without** the permission of the court where proceedings have been struck out on the following grounds:

- ➤ C has disclosed no reasonable grounds for bringing the proceedings, or
- ➤ The proceedings are an abuse of the court's process, or
- ➤ The conduct of C is likely to obstruct the just disposal of proceedings

---

[82] s 44 LASPO 2012

Second qualification – C fundamentally dishonest

Under CPR 44.16, orders for costs against C may be fully enforced with the permission of the court where the claim is found on the balance of probabilities to be fundamentally dishonest.

22.4. Private funding – DBAs

Similar to CFAs, a DBA is a 'no win, no fee' agreement. The core difference is that when C enters into a DBA and C wins, C's legal representative will receive a percentage of C's general damages (instead of a percentage uplift on costs).

There is a 'prescribed amount' of C's general damages. DBAs cannot provide for payment of more than the **prescribed amount**. The amount is 50% of C's award in a non-PI case and 25% of general damages awarded in a PI case.

A DBA is enforceable if it:
> Is in writing,
> Does not relate to proceedings which cannot be the subject of an enforceable CFA, and
> Its terms and conditions comply with prescribed requirements

22.5. Summary and detailed assessment

Summary assessment

In summary assessment the court determines the costs payable immediately after the end of the substantive hearing. The court will work through the Statement of Costs (served 24 hours prior to the hearing) on an item-by-item basis. It will generally approach calculations roughly.

Summary assessment should occur at the end of the trial unless there is good reason not to do so.[83]

---

[83] PD 44 [9.2]

Costs are generally payable within 14 days of the date of the order although the court retains a discretion.[84]

Detailed assessment

In detailed assessment the court leaves the assessment of costs to a costs judge. The amount of costs will then be considered at an assessment hearing within 3 months from the date of judgment. Detailed assessments are carried out by DJs in a county court and by judges in the Senior Courts Cost Office in the High Court.

Detailed assessment is mandatory where:
> Money is claimed for the benefit of a child or protected party[85]
> A party has been publicly funded[86]

Detailed assessment of costs is likely to be ordered for multi-track cases running into multiple days or weeks.

22.6. Standard and indemnity bases

The standard basis is the method usually applied in calculating costs orders. It acts to restrict the total costs award. By contrast, the indemnity basis is a less restrictive calculation method. The indemnity basis may be adopted where:
> The court seeks to penalize a party for misconduct during litigation, or
> Trustee costs are payable out of the trust fund, or
> C recovers more at trial than the amount offered by D in a Part 36 offer (see Chapter 20)

Standard basis

Under the standard basis, the court will only allow costs that are:
> Reasonably incurred and are reasonable in amount, and
> Proportionate to the matters in issue

---

[84] CPR 44.7(1)
[85] CPR 46.4
[86] PD 44 [9.8]

Any doubt in determining whether costs are reasonable incurred, reasonable in amount or proportionate to the matters in issue is resolved in favour of the paying party.[87]

Indemnity basis
Under the indemnity basis, the court will only allow costs that are:
> ➤ Reasonably incurred and are reasonable in amount

There is no requirement that costs must be proportionate. Any doubt in determining whether costs are reasonably incurred or are reasonable in amount is resolved in favour of the receiving party.[88]

22.7. Interim costs orders and their effects: PD 44 [4.2]

Costs of an interim application are in the discretion of the court. The discretion is usually exercised in favour of the successful party in the application.

Under CPR 44.10(1) if an order makes no reference to costs the general rule is that none are payable for the proceedings to which the order relates. There are exceptions for trustees, landlords and mortgages, and applications made without notice.

---

[87] CPR 44.3(1) – (2)
[88] CPR 44.3(1) and (3)

Order	Effect[89]
Costs / Costs in any event	The successful party in the interim application is entitled to his costs for the proceedings to which the order relates, regardless of other costs orders for the rest of proceedings.
Costs in the case / Costs in the application	The successful party in the interim application is entitled to his costs for the proceedings to which the order relates.
Costs reserved	The costs decision is deferred to a later occasion. If no later order is made, costs will be costs in the case.
C's / D's costs in the case/application	If the successful party in the interim application also succeeds overall, that party is entitled to its costs of the proceedings to which the order relates.
Costs thrown away	Where a judgment or order is set aside, the successful party in the interim application is entitled to the costs incurred as a consequence.
Costs of and caused by	Following an application to amend a statement of case, A will bear the costs of R preparing for and attending the application, and the costs of consequential amendment.
Costs here and below	The successful party in the interim application is entitled to its costs for that application but also its costs from the proceedings in any lower court.[90]
No order as to costs / each party to pay his own costs	Each party bears its own costs for the application.[91]

---

[89] PD 44 [4.2]
[90] Not applicable where application is made in Divisional Court
[91] Subject to CPR 44.10(2) exceptions

22.8. Situations where costs do not follow the event: CPR 44.2(3) – (4)

In deciding whether the costs order should follow the event, a court will have regard to all the circumstances, including:

- The **conduct** of the parties, which includes:
  - o Conduct before and during proceedings
  - o Whether it was reasonable to raise a particular allegation
  - o The manner in which the case has been pursued, and
  - o Any exaggeration by the successful party of its claim
- Whether the party has been **wholly or partly successful**, and
- Any admissible **offers to settle** (e.g. an offer made without prejudice save as to costs) (see Chapter 20.4)

If a costs order is to be made the court must quantify costs. First the court will decide the basis to be used. Then the court will have regard to a number of factors when calculating the appropriate amount.[92] The factors include the conduct of the parties, amounts of money involved, complexity of the issues and the extent of specialised knowledge required.

Wasted Costs Orders: CPR 46.8 and PD 46 [5.5]

A **legal representative** may be ordered by a court to meet 'wasted costs', where the court considers:

- The legal representative has acted improperly, unreasonably or negligently,
- The legal representative has caused a party to incur unnecessary costs, and
- It is just in all the circumstances to make the order

22.9. Likely costs order where party has partial success

Generally, when a party is partially successful, the trial judge will award one party only a percentage of their costs. This saves the

---

[92] CPR 44.4(3)

unnecessary complexity of awarding costs on different issues to different parties.[93]

22.10. Likely costs order where C succeeds against some but not all Ds

The court has the discretion to make a *Bullock* or *Sanderson* Order.

Bullock Order

Where C succeeds against D2 but fails against D1, C will be ordered to pay D1's costs. D2 is ordered to pay C's costs and then also reimburse C for having to pay D1's costs.

Sanderson Order

Following the same part success / part failure, D2 is ordered to pay C's costs and D1's costs directly. C has no liability to pay D1's costs.

When choosing between orders, the court will look at all the facts including whether C knew or reasonably could have discovered when D2 was joined and consider whether the joinder was reasonable.

22.11. Public funding

Likely costs orders if one or more parties are publically funded

If a publicly funded party succeeds the court will make an order for costs on exactly the same principles as in unassisted cases. Quantification must also be calculated as if the party was not publicly funded. Recovered costs are used to first of all pay the LAA.

If a publicly funded party is unsuccessful the party itself remains protected from the usual costs consequences.[94]

Under s 26(1) LASPO 2012, the costs ordered against a publicly funded party must not exceed the amount which it is reasonable for the individual to pay having regard to all the circumstances, including:

---

[93] *English v Emery Reimbold and Strick Ltd* [2002] EWCA Civ 605
[94] s 26 LASPO 2012

- The financial resources of all the parties to the proceedings, and
- Their conduct during the dispute

Statutory charge

A publicly funded party who succeeds in proceedings may recover money or assets. The recovery will be subject to a statutory charge under s 25 LASPO 2012. This charge only applies if there remains a net liability to the LAA. Since public funding is treated as a loan rather than a gift, that liability will usually exist in this situation.

Where a party is publicly funded, there must be a detailed assessment of costs at the end of proceedings.

Counsel's duty to the LAA:

It may be appropriate for counsel to advise the LAA that public funding be withdrawn or evaluated if:
- The client requires counsel to conduct the case in an unreasonable manner
- Facts come to light which persuade counsel that an arguable case no longer exists, or
- There is a change in the party's circumstances

22.12. Costs orders in pro bono cases

Where a party who has received pro bono representation has succeeded the court retains the power to order costs to be paid by the losing side to a prescribed charity.[95] The amount to be paid can be no more than what would have been paid had the party had not received pro bono representation.

---

[95] CPR 46.7(4)

CHAPTER SUMMARY

> The general rule in costs is that 'costs follow the event', but this remains subject to the discretion of the court.

> QOCS is not an absolute rule and a C in a PI claim cannot abuse the costs protection mechanism.

> Detailed assessments are mandatory in some instances and discretionary in others.

23. JUDGMENTS AND ORDERS

Whether proposed by consenting parties or imposed upon them, a judgment or order binds litigants.

23.1. Responsibility for drawing up a judgment / order

The general rule: CPR 40.3(1)
The general rule is that every judgment or order will be drawn up by **the court** unless the an exception applies.

Exceptions
The general rule will not apply where:[96]
> ➤ The court orders a party to draw it up
> ➤ A party, with the permission of the court, agrees to draw it up
> ➤ The court dispenses with the need to draw it up
> ➤ It is a Consent Order under CPR 40.6, or
> ➤ The claim is proceeding in the QBD (other than the Administrative Court). In the QBD every judgment or order will be drawn up by the parties (except when the court makes an order of its own initiative)

Power to check
The court may still direct that:[97]
> ➤ A judgment or order drawn up by a party must first be checked by the court before it is sealed, or
> ➤ Before a judgment or order is drawn up by the court, the parties must file an agreed statement of terms

Timing
If a party is going to draw up an order the party has 7 days from the court order to draw it up.

---

[96] CPR 40.3(1)(a)-(d) and CPR 40.3(4)
[97] CPR 40.3(2)

Requirements for a judgment: CPR 40.2

Every judgment or order **must**:

- ➢ Be sealed by the court
- ➢ State the name and judicial title of the person who made it (subject to exceptions, e.g. *Tomlin* orders are made by court officers)
- ➢ State the date on which it is given
- ➢ State whether or not the judgment / order is final
- ➢ State whether an appeal lies from the judgment / order and (if so) which appeal court, and
- ➢ State whether the court gives permission to appeal (and if not, state the appropriate appeal court for the further application for permission to appeal)

23.2. Consequence of failing to draw up and file a judgment / order within the time permitted: CPR 40.3(1)(b)

Where a judgment or order is to be drawn up by a party, if she fails to file it within the 7 day period, **any other party** may draw it up and file it.

23.3. The time for payment of a money judgment

Money judgments: CPR 40.11

A money judgment must be paid within 14 days of the date of the judgment, unless:

- ➢ The judgment specifies a different date (e.g. instalments), or
- ➢ The CPR specifies a different date (for example, with certain default judgments), or
- ➢ The court stays proceedings

Judgments requiring acts to be done: PD 40B [8.1]

A judgment or order that requires an act to be done, other than an act in the form of the payment of an amount of money, must **specify** the time within which the act should be done.

23.4. Penal notices in interim injunction orders: Section 2, PD 81

The failure to adhere to interim injunction orders may result in proceedings for contempt of court and ultimately imprisonment or fine.

A prohibitory or mandatory interim injunction order **must**, if disobedience is to be dealt with by proceedings for contempt of court, have a penal notice endorsed on it.[98]

The form of the penal notice

'If you the within-named [.........] do not comply with this order you may be held to be in contempt of court and imprisoned or fined, or your assets may be seized.'

23.5. *Tomlin* orders: CPR 40.6.2

Definition

A *Tomlin* Order is a type of Consent Order. This is reflected in the sub-heading in a *Tomlin* Order: *'It is by consent ordered that'*. A *Tomlin* Order records the terms of a settlement agreed between the parties. Such an order becomes necessary where terms of settlement exceed the court's jurisdiction.

Contents of the terms within the order and the schedule

The terms of a *Tomlin* Order are effectively divided into two distinct parts: the order itself and the schedule attached to it.[99]

The terms recorded within the order are restricted to the issues the court has jurisdiction over (the main issues between the parties in the case and costs). The order will also confirm that all further proceedings shall be stayed except for the purpose of carrying the terms in the schedule into effect and that there is liberty to apply as to carrying such terms into effect.

---

[98] PD 81 [1], but note CPR 81.9(2)
[99] CPR 40.6(7)

Terms within the schedule do not form part of the order. They cannot be directly enforced as an order of the court because the schedule contains agreement on issues outside the court's jurisdiction (issues it was never asked to adjudicate). In the schedule the parties have made an agreement on terms outside the remit of the court.

Pre-conditions for a *Tomlin* Order
In order for a court officer to enter and seal a *Tomlin* Order, the court officer must be satisfied that none of the parties is a litigant in person and that the court's approval is not required by the CPR or legislation.

Effect of a *Tomlin* Order
A *Tomlin* Order has the effect of staying the claim save for the purpose of carrying the terms set out in a schedule to the order into effect.

Enforcing the terms of the schedule
The schedule contains a binding contract between the parties. If any of the terms in the schedule are breached enforcement is two-stage process. First the claim must be restored (since it has been stayed) using the 'liberty to apply' clause. An order must be sought from the court to compel compliance with the relevant term. Second, once that order is breached, enforcement is through the usual method (see Chapter 24).

Grounds for setting aside or varying a *Tomlin* Order
There are two categories of cases where a *Tomlin* Order may be set aside or varied:
- ➤ Cases in which there was, at the date of the order, an erroneous basis of fact, and
- ➤ Cases in which there has been a material or unforeseen change in circumstances after the order to undermine or invalidate the order's basis[100]

---

[100] *S v S (Ancillary Relief: Consent Order)* [2002] 1 FLR 992

23.6. Orders requiring an act to be done: PD 40B [8]

An order requiring an act to be done (other than a judgment or order for the payment of money) must specify the time within which the act should be done.

The consequences of failure to do an act within the time specified may be set out in the order.[101] In such a case, very specific language must be used:

> *'Unless C/D serves his list of documents by [time] on [date], his Claim/Defence shall/will be struck out and judgment entered for D/C.'*

If a party fails to comply with an 'unless order', the relevant statement of case 'shall / will' be struck out in accordance with the order. In the context of strike out, if the party fails to comply with the unless order, an opposition party may simply obtain judgment with costs by filing a request for judgment using a CPR 23 application notice.[102] The defaulting party may apply to set the judgment aside within 14 days of the judgment.[103]

CHAPTER SUMMARY
> ➢ The general rule is that the court will draw up the judgment or order.
> ➢ Injunctions should contain penal notices.
> ➢ *Tomlin* Orders are separated into two distinct parts. The schedule does not form part of the order and is enforced through a different mechanism.

---

[101] PD 40B [8.2]
[102] CPR 3.5
[103] CPR 3.6

24. ENFORCEMENT OF JUDGMENTS

There are a number of different methods of enforcing judgments. It is important to consider them well in advance of obtaining a judgment or else it may be too late to receive payment.

A judgment creditor 'JC' is someone who has obtained judgment against a judgment debtor 'JD'.

24.1. Different methods of enforcement

Where a number of enforcement methods are available, a judgment creditor can choose whichever method(s) seems likely to be the most effective. Each method is designed to deal with a particular circumstance. In outline, they are:
  ➢ Obtaining information from debtors
  ➢ Execution against goods
  ➢ Administration orders
  ➢ Third party debt orders
  ➢ Attachment of earnings
  ➢ Charging orders
  ➢ Bankruptcy or winding up proceedings
  ➢ Judgment summons

24.2. Preliminary: transfer

A case may need to be transferred before enforcement proceedings are commenced.

From	To	**Must** be transferred if JC seeks:
County Court	High Court	➤ Execution against goods > £5,000,[104] or ➤ Enforcement of a charging order by sale where the amount sought > £30,000[105]
High Court	County Court	➤ Execution against goods of a judgment for < £600,[106] ➤ A charging order where the judgment debt is < £5,000,[107] or ➤ An attachment of earnings order[108]
Another County Court	The county court serving JD's district	➤ Information from a JD or a TP debt order in a designated money claim, ➤ A charging order, or ➤ An attachment of earnings order

24.3. Obtaining information from JDs: CPR 71

Where there is insufficient information on JD's finances an application can be made to obtain that information. The court will order JD to attend for questioning.

A specific application notice must be used to apply for the order.
The application notice must:
> ➤ State JD's name and address
> ➤ Identify the judgment

---

[104] Art 8(1)(a) High Court and County Court Jurisdiction Order 1991. This does not apply to regulated agreements under the Consumer Credit Act 1974
[105] s 23(c) County Courts Act 1984
[106] Art 8(1)(b) High Court and County Court Jurisdiction Order 1991
[107] s 1(2) Charging Orders Act 1979
[108] s 1 Attachment of Earnings Act 1971

- ➤ State the amount presently owing under the judgment, and
- ➤ If specific documents are sought (e.g. bank statements), these must be specified[109]

Timeline of procedural steps:

Step	Comment
Order to attend	On receipt of the application, a court officer will make an order requiring JD to attend court, produce documents and answer questions
Service of order	The order must be served personally on JD no less than 14 days before the hearing
Reasonable sum for travelling expenses	JD then has 7 days to ask JC for a reasonable sum to cover JD's travelling expenses to court (these must be paid)
Affidavit by JC	JC has to swear an **affidavit** indicating the sum outstanding
Filing of affidavit	The affidavit must be filed 2 days before the hearing or produced at the hearing
Hearing	At the hearing, the court officer will ask a standard set of questions[110]

24.4. Execution against goods

This is the most common form of enforcement.

In the High Court, the order is called a **Writ of Fieri Facias** (also known as 'fi.fa'). In a county court, the order is called a **Warrant of Execution**.

---

[109] PD 71 [1.2]
[110] PD 71

Timeline of enforcement steps:

Step	Comment
Lawful entry	The enforcement officers or bailiffs must gain lawful entry to JD's premises.

Seizure of goods	Sufficient goods will then be seized to satisfy the judgment and the costs of enforcement.
	
	This **cannot** include:
	  ➤ Tools or equipment necessary to JD for use in JD's employment / business
	  ➤ Items necessary to the basic domestic needs of JD and JD's family
	
	A JD claiming goods fall into either of these excluded categories must give notice to the sheriff within 5 days of seizure.

Walking possession	An agreement that the goods will remain at JD's premises until payment or sale may be agreed with a 'responsible person'.

24.5. Administration orders

A county court has power (of its own motion or on application) to make an Administration Order in respect of JD's estate.[111] The order will usually provide for JD to make specified payments by instalments.

24.6. TP debt orders: CPR 72 and PD 72

The order results in a debt payable by a TP to JD becoming payable instead to the JC. This is particularly useful where TP is a bank.

---

[111] s 112 County Courts Act 1984

Enforcement is a **two-stage process**:
- ➤ JC makes an application without notice for an interim TP debt order
- ➤ There is then a hearing on notice for a final order

Timeline of procedural steps:

Step	Comment
Evidence of bank account	Orders will only be made if there is evidence to substantiate a belief that the debtor has an account with the bank
Without notice hearing	The judge will fix a date for a final hearing
Service of interim order on TP	The interim order granted must be served on the third party not less than 21 days before the final hearing date
TP search	TP must carry out a search and disclose the relevant information
Service of interim order on JD	The interim order must be served on JD not less than 7 days after TP is served
Final hearing	At the final hearing the court may: ➤ Make a final TP debt order ➤ Discharge the interim order ➤ Decide any issues ➤ Direct a trial of any issues

An interim order **binds** a TP to freeze any debts due to JD up to the amount of the judgment debt.

24.7. Attachment of earnings: Attachment of Earnings Act 1971

Where a JD is employed but has no other substantial assets the most appropriate form of enforcement is to obtain an attachment of earnings order. This acts to instruct JD's employer to deduct periodical sums from JD's attachable earnings.

Attachable earnings	Non-attachable earnings
➢ Wages, salaries, fees, bonuses, commission and overtime ➢ Occupational pensions ➢ Statutory sick pay	➢ Self employed income ➢ State pensions / benefits / allowances

Timeline of procedural steps:

Step	Comment
Application notice	A standard application notice is filed stating the amount due under the judgment
JD notified	The court notifies JD of the hearing date at least 21 days in advance
Financial means questionnaire	JD fills out a questionnaire on his financial means
Hearing	A DJ will consider JD's income and expenses at a hearing
Protected earnings rate and normal deduction rate	The DJ sets a **protected earnings rate** (to allow JD to live) and a **normal deduction rate** (deducted from JD's earnings per week / month)
Order served on JD's employer	The order will be served on JD's employer who will make the deductions and then pay them to the court

24.8. Charging orders: CPR 73

A charge is a form of security over property (a mortgage is a type of charge). A charging order secures a judgment debt by imposing a charge on JD's property.[112] A charging order does **not** of itself produce payment but acts to secure a judgment debt.

Chargeable property includes any interest held by the debtor beneficially, including:
- ➢ Land
- ➢ Securities and stocks, and
- ➢ Funds in court

Similar to TP debt orders, enforcement is a **two-stage process**:
- ➢ JC makes an application notice for an interim charging order
- ➢ The court awards a final charging order at the second hearing

Timeline of procedural steps:

Step	Comment
Application notice	An application notice is submitted by JC seeking an interim charging order
Hearing fixed	The application is initially dealt with without a hearing: a hearing is fixed to consider making a final charging order
Service of interim order on JD	JD must be served with the interim charging order at least 21 days before the final hearing date

24.9. Bankruptcy or winding up proceedings

Often a failure to pay a judgment debt is evidence that JD is insolvent. In such a case it may be suitable to bring bankruptcy or winding up proceedings.

---

[112] s 1(1) Charging Orders Act 1979

24.10. Judgment summons

Judgment summons is a procedure for imprisoning a defaulting JD who could pay but has chosen not to. It is **only** available for enforcing matrimonial maintenance orders and some tax arrears.

CHAPTER SUMMARY

> There are different monetary values at which cases must be transferred between county courts and the High Court.
> Execution against goods remains the most common form of enforcement.
> Enforcement is a two-stage process for both third party orders and charging orders.
> The choice of enforcement method is decided through examining the particular circumstances. The important questions are where JD's assets are located and which enforcement method is best suited to enforcing against those assets.

25. JUDICIAL REVIEW

Judicial review ('JR') is not an appeal from a decision but instead a review of the manner in which the decision was made. The purpose of JR is to ensure that an individual is given fair treatment by a public body.

In this chapter 'A' is the party making the application for JR and 'R' is the party responding to application.

25.1. Scope of JR

Applications for JR **must** be brought in the High Court (Administrative Court of the QBD).

Parties
JR will lie against any body charged with the performance of a public duty. This includes inferior courts and tribunals.

Standing
An A seeking JR must have 'a sufficient interest in the matter to which the application relates'. A personal interest in the decision will be sufficient.

Public law
An A complaining of an infringement of public law rights must proceed by way of JR rather than by ordinary claim.

25.2. Permission to claim JR: CPR 54

The purpose of obtaining permission is to remove frivolous applications so the court can focus on more meritorious cases.

Persons intending to apply for JR should generally comply with the Pre-Action Protocol: JR before applying.

Timeline of procedural steps

Step	Comment
Letter before Claim from A	A should send a letter of claim to R seeking to establish whether JR can be avoided and identifying the issues.
Reply by R (or interim reply by R)	R should reply within 14 days. Where R cannot reply within this time, an interim reply should be sent back to A proposing a reasonable extension
Service of Claim Form	Under CPR 54.7, the JR Claim Form and all other documentation must be served on the R and all other interested parties within 7 days after the date of issue.
Granting permission to proceed	The papers are considered by a judge without a hearing. Permission is granted where there is an arguable case for granting the relief claimed. If refused, A may file a request for the decision to be reconsidered at a hearing. This must be made within 7 days of service of the refusal.
Substantive Hearing	If permission is granted, A and R may make submissions.

Time limit for filing the Claim Form: CPR 54.5(1)
The Claim Form initiating an application for JR must be filed promptly, and in any event, not later than 3 months after the grounds to make the claim arose. An application can still be refused for delay if it has not been made **promptly** even if it is made within 3 months.

Contents of the JR Claim Form: CPR 54.6 and PD 54A
A JR Claim Form must state:
> - The name and address of any person A considers to be an interested party
> - That A is requesting permission to proceed with a claim for judicial review
> - A's grounds for bringing the judicial review claim in detail
> - A statement of the facts relied upon
> - Any remedy that is being claimed, and
> - Any relief sought under the HRA 1998 and if so, precise details of the convention right alleged to have been infringed

25.3. Substantive hearing

If A successfully obtains permission for JR there will be a substantive hearing before a HCJ.

25.4. Remedies in JR

There are six remedies available on applications for JR. The various forms of relief may be claimed either in the alternative or in addition as long as they arise out of the same issue or matter.

Quashing order *(previously 'certiorari')*
A quashing order annuls the decision of an inferior court or public authority. It usually means that the matter is remitted with a direction for the lower court, tribunal or public authority to reach a new decision.

Mandatory order *(previously 'mandamus')*
A mandatory order requires an inferior court or public authority to carry out its duties. This is applicable where the body is guilty of wrongful inaction (such as a refusal to exercise a discretion).

Prohibiting order *(previously 'prohibition')*
A prohibiting order restrains an inferior court or public authority from acting outside of its jurisdiction. An A does not have to wait for a public body to exercise its jurisdiction before applying but may apply to prevent a public body from doing a certain act before the public body

has done it.

Injunction

An injunction is a mandatory or prohibiting order designed to prevent an action/activity continuing. It is noted that this remedy cannot be ordered against the Crown under English law. An injunction may only be granted where the court considers it just and convenient to do so.

Declaration

The court makes a declaration by answering a question of law or rights. It remains a discretionary remedy. In the same way as an injunction, it is granted only where the court considers it just and convenient to do so.

Money award

A court can order an award of damages, restitution, or the recovery of a sum due. However, such a remedy does not survive on its own: it can only be made in conjunction with another judicial remedy.

CHAPTER SUMMARY

> ➢ Prior to attending court for a JR hearing permission to proceed must be sought and attained.
> ➢ In the same way as Part 7 claims parties are expected to follow the guidance provided by the JR pre-action protocol.

26. APPEALS

A party who has lost at a hearing may in limited circumstances appeal the decision. Appeals are expensive and may require permission of the court.

In this chapter 'A' is the party making the application to appeal and 'R' is the party responding to the appeal.

26.1. Permission to appeal: CPR 52.3

General rule and exceptions: CPR 52.3(1)
The starting position is that A requires permission to appeal from a decision of a county court judge or HCJ. Permission is not required where the appeal is against:
- ➤ A committal order
- ➤ A refusal to grant habeas corpus
- ➤ A secure accommodation order[113]

Conditions to appeal: CPR 52.3(6)
In order to appeal a decision, A must show:[114]
- ➤ The appeal would have a real prospect of success, or
- ➤ There is some other compelling reason for an appeal

Where to apply
The application is made:
- ➤ To the lower court at the hearing to be appealed, or
- ➤ To the appeal court in an appeal notice

---

[113] s 25 Children Act 1989
[114] Note the similarity to the test for summary judgment: see Chapter 13.6

Refusals

If a court refuses permission to appeal, further applications can be made:

Step	Comment
Lower court refuses application to appeal	A may make a further application to the appeal court.
Appeal court refuses A's application without a hearing	A may apply within 7 days for a reconsideration at a hearing

26.2. Routes of appeal

General route of appeal

The 'appeal court' is not the same for every appeal. In general, appeal lies to the next level of judge. The notable exception is for any Part 7 claim in final proceedings on the multi-track, which is appealed to the CA.[115] This is shown in grey in the table over page.

The routes of appeal are as follows on the table over the page:

---

[115] Art 4(a) Access to Justice Act 1990 (Destination of Appeals) Order 2000

Court being appealed	Level of judge being appealed	Type of claim and track being appealed	Type of proceedings being appealed	Appeal court and judge
County Court	DJ	Part 7 / 8	Interim / Final	CJ (County Court)
		Part 7 (multi-track)	Final	CA
	CJ	Part 7 / 8	Interim / Final	HCJ
		Part 7 (multi-track)	Final	CA

Court being appealed	Level of judge being appealed	Type of claim and track being appealed	Type of proceedings being appealed	Appeal court and judge
High Court	Master	Part 7 / 8	Interim / Final	HCL
		Part 7 (multi-track)	Final	CA
	HCJ	Any	Interim / Final	CA

A final decision is a decision that finally disposes of proceedings (e.g. trial) but does not include summary judgment or strike out.

Second appeals (appealing from a decision on appeal)
Second appeals must be made in the CA (unless appealing the CA to the SC).[116]

A second appeal will be allowed if:
- ➤ There is an important point of principle or practice
- ➤ There is some other compelling reason

26.3. Time for appealing (Appellant's notice): CPR 52.4(2)(b)

A must seek permission to appeal in her Appellant's notice. The notice must be:
- ➤ Filed with the appeal court
- ➤ Within the time period as directed by the lower court (if there is no direction, within 21 days of the decision being appealed)
- ➤ Served on each R as soon as practicable (and in any event, within 7 days of filing with the court)

Variation of these time limits can only be done by application to the appeal court.[117] The consent of A and R will not be sufficient.

26.4. Grounds for appeal: CPR 52.11

A may only appeal on the grounds that the decision was:
- ➤ Wrong in law
- ➤ Wrong in fact
- ➤ Wrong in the exercise of discretion
- ➤ Unjust because of a serious procedural defect or other irregularity

The appeal court may draw any inference of fact that it considers justified.

26.5. Fresh evidence

There is no oral evidence in an appeal. The general rule is that there can be no fresh evidence, that is, no evidence that was not before the lower court.

---

[116] Art 5 Access to Justice Act 1990 (Destination of Appeals) Order 2000
[117] CPR 52.6(1)

However, fresh evidence can be used on appeal if:[118]
> The evidence could not have been obtained with reasonable diligence for use at the hearing, **and**
> The evidence would have had an important influence on the result of the case (although not necessarily decisive), **and**
> The evidence is apparently credible

26.6. Respondent's notice

A Respondent's notice must be filed when R is:[119]
> Appealing from the appeal court
> Appealing to the appeal court to uphold the lower court for different or additional reasons

Timing

The Respondent's notice should be filed with the appeal court in the time directed by the lower court. If no time is given, then depending on the way the appeal was granted, R should file within 14 days from:
> R being served with A's notice (where permission to appeal was given by the lower court)
> R being notified that the appeal court has given A permission to appeal
> The date R was notified that A's application to appeal and the appeal itself will be heard together

The Respondent's notice should be served on each A and R as soon as practicable and in any event, not more than 7 days after filing with the court.

26.7. Skeleton arguments

Whether skeleton arguments are required is subject to any order of the court. The usual rule is that skeleton arguments are only required where:

---

[118] *Ladd v Marshall* [1954] 1 WLR 1489
[119] CPR 52.5(2)

- ➤ The appeal is in the CA
- ➤ There are complex issues of fact or law
- ➤ A skeleton would assist the court in a was that is not obvious from the other documents

Content of a skeleton argument

The skeleton argument is to assist the court in case management. It should contain references to the appeal bundle.

It should contain a summary of the party's submissions. It should not be more than 25 pages long and must justify the reason if giving more than one authority per point of law. There may be cost consequences for non-compliance.

26.8. Stays of execution pending appeal

Unless the lower court or the appeal court orders otherwise an appeal does not operate as a stay of any order. The party who won in the lower court is entitled to the judgment or order and it can be enforced.

If the losing party applies for a stay the court will consider if there is a risk of injustice if the stay is granted.

CHAPTER SUMMARY
- ➤ If a party seeks to appeal a judgment of a lower court, she should initially make the application for permission to appeal to the lower court.
- ➤ The route for appeals is usually to the next level of judge, apart from final Part 7 claims on the Multi-Track which are appealed to the CA.
- ➤ There are limited grounds for appeal.

27. CIVIL EVIDENCE

The diverse areas covered have been grouped into four headings:
- ➤ Proof, Hearsay and Previous Judgments
- ➤ Witnesses
- ➤ Expert Evidence
- ➤ Legal Professional Privilege

PROOF, HEARSAY AND PREVIOUS JUDGMENTS

27.1. Burden and standard of proof

Burden of proof
The burden or proof is the requirement of a party to produce sufficient evidence to persuade the court. In English law C bears the burden of proof. If C fails to prove her case, her claim will fail.

Standard of proof
The standard of proof is what level of evidence C must show in order to discharge the burden of proof. The usual standard is 'more probable than not'. Exceptions to the standard are made when:
- ➤ Required by statute, or
- ➤ There are criminal implications (e.g. contempt proceedings) where the criminal standard ('sure') will be used

If C is alleging fraud the **normal standard will apply,** but as fraud is an improbable event, strong evidence will be required.

27.2. Hearsay evidence

Hearsay evidence is **admissible** in civil proceedings by virtue of <u>s 1(1) Civil Evidence Act 1995</u> ('<u>CEA 1995</u>').

Definition: <u>s 1(2) CEA 1995</u>
A hearsay statement is:
- ➤ A statement

> Not made in oral evidence in civil proceedings to which the strict rules of evidence apply
> Tendered as evidence of the matter stated

Strict rules of evidence do not apply in the small claims court or in tribunals.

A statement is tendered as evidence of the matter stated if the statement must be true in order to be relevant.

Procedural requirements

If a statement is hearsay evidence then in some cases procedural requirements must be met before it can be relied upon.

The table over the page shows the types of hearsay statement.

There are three types of hearsay statement:[120]

	Definition	Procedure
Type 1	Hearsay evidence will be given orally	> Give notice by serving W/S
Type 2	Hearsay evidence in W/S, but W not available to attend court	> Give notice by serving W/S > Inform other party that W will not attend > Give a reason for absence
Type 3	All other cases	> Serve a notice that identifies the hearsay > State that party intends to rely upon hearsay

As W/S will normally be exchanged, Type 1 hearsay involves no additional procedural step.

---

[120] Credit to Alexandra Frith of University of Law for this division

Failure to comply with procedure
A failure to comply does not render the hearsay inadmissible. However, the court may:
- ➢ Refuse to allow the costs of the evidence
- ➢ Attach less weight to the evidence

Options available to a party served with a hearsay notice
A party served with a hearsay notice can:
- ➢ Request particulars of the evidence
- ➢ Make submissions aimed at reducing the weight to be attached to the evidence, which may include:
  - o Whether the original statement was made at the same time as another matter
  - o The motive of the maker of the statement
  - o In a Type 2 case, whether W should have been present given the size of the case and difficulty of being present

In a Type 2 case, a party may additionally:
- ➢ Apply to XX the maker of the W/S with **permission** (the application can only be made where W has no good reason for absence)
- ➢ Call evidence to attack the maker's credibility (no permission is required, but notice to attack is needed)

The application and / or notice must be made within 14 days of service of the hearsay notice.

Exceptions: inadmissibility of hearsay
A hearsay statement will be inadmissible if:
- ➢ The reporter / listener to the statement was not competent at the time they reported it. This means a mental or physical infirmity or a lack of understanding, or
- ➢ The statement is opinion evidence (see Chapter 27.7 below)

27.3. Previous judgments: *res judicata* and abuse of process

The general rule is that parties cannot re-litigate an issue decided by a competent court. Parties should present the whole of their case at the first opportunity. The principle is that legal certainty requires an end to litigation.

The related doctrines of *res judicata*, abuse of process, cause of action and issue estoppel will prevent a litigant in a second claim who wishes to:
> ➢ Challenge adverse findings in earlier proceedings, or
> ➢ Bring new claim that could or should have been brought in earlier proceedings

Abuse of process is a wider doctrine, but will depend on all the circumstances. Where *res judicata* does not apply the court has the power under CPR 3.4 to strike out new proceedings as an abuse of process if:
> ➢ It would be manifestly unfair to a party in a later claim for the issues to be re-litigated, or
> ➢ Re-litigating will bring the administration of justice into disrepute

WITNESSES

The use of witnesses ('Ws') and witness statements ('W/S') is often crucial to court proceedings.

27.4. Competence and compellability of Ws

Competence
The general rule is that all Ws are competent to give evidence.

Exceptions to competence
There are two exceptions:
> Children
> Persons with defective intellect, such that they are
>> o Prevented from understanding the nature of the oath, and
>> o Prevent from giving rational testimony

Children are competent if they:[121]
> Understand their duty to speak the truth, and
> Have sufficient understanding to justify the evidence being heard

The court will decide on their competence.

Compellability
The general rule is that all competent Ws are compellable. A W can be compelled to give oral evidence at court or produce a document.

If W is compelled to attend court, a witness summons will be required. The party requesting the summons will usually have it granted as a matter of course, but court permission is required if summoning W:
> Less that 7 days before trial, or
> For any hearing other than a trial

---

[121] s 96 Children Act 1989

A separate summons is required for each W. The summons will offer W a sum of compensation for attending.

Failure to obey a witness summons

A W who fails to obey a witness summons may face a fine of up to £1,000 in the county court and committal for contempt in the High Court.

27.5. Preparation and exchange of W/S

As noted in Chapter 14, the court will normally direct that the exchange of W/S be simultaneous.

Sanction for late service

If a W/S is served late then:

➢ The W/S is not admissible
➢ The party in breach may not rely upon that W
➢ The party in breach may not receive costs of preparing the W/S
➢ The party in breach must apply for relief from sanctions under CPR 3.9

Content of W/S

A W/S should be written in the first person, and set out the material events in chronological order.

The opening paragraph should set out:

➢ The occupation of W
➢ Where W resides
➢ Whether W is a party to proceedings
➢ Whether W makes the statement in a professional or official capacity

The W/S should identify whether a matter is based on belief or information and give the source. It should not be used for legal argument.

Use of W/S
The general rule is that:
> ➢ Evidence at trial is proved by oral evidence
> ➢ Evidence at other hearings is proved by written evidence

However, a W/S stands as a W's XIC unless the court orders otherwise. W will be asked to confirm that she has read her statement and is content for it to stand as her evidence. W may amplify her statement or give evidence on new matters with the permission of the court.

This means that in practice most of the time at trials is spent on XX of Ws. A party who has served a W/S must call the W unless the court orders otherwise.

At hearings other than trial, evidence is by W/S unless otherwise ordered, although a statement of case and application notice can be relied upon as evidence if verified by a statement of truth (see Chapter 6.4).

Collateral use of W/S is not permitted unless:
> ➢ All parties consent
> ➢ The court allows the use by court order
> ➢ The W/S has been put in evidence at a public hearing

Form of W/S
A W/S is a document for the court and the same formal requirements as applied to statements of case apply (see Chapter 6.3). A W/S should be signed with a **statement of truth**.

The W/S should be headed with the formal heading of the claim. At the top right-hand side the following should appear:
> ➢ The name of the party on whose behalf it is made
> ➢ The initials and surname of W
> ➢ The date of the statement

Any reference to an exhibit must either be in the margins or in bold.

Affidavits and witness summaries

An affidavit is a statement made under oath and witnessed. Affidavits are required for:

> ➤ Search orders
> ➤ Freezing injunctions
> ➤ Orders requiring an occupier to permit another the enter their land

When not required, affidavits can be used instead of W/S, but the additional costs of an affidavit will not be recoverable.

If a signed W/S cannot be served in time, a witness summary can be filed.

27.6. Cross Examination ('XX') and Evidence in Chief ('XIC')

In civil trials a W/S stands as W's XIC unless the court orders otherwise.

Leading and non-leading questions

The most important difference between XX and XIC is that leading questions may (and should) be asked in XX. There are restrictions on XX as to credit: see Chapter 27.8.

Rule of (collateral) finality

In order to avoid lengthy proceedings, an answer given by W on a matter not directly relevant to the facts in issue (a collateral matter) is final. A party may not adduce evidence to prove the contrary, but that party is not required to accept W's account.

Exceptions to the rule of collateral finality

The following exceptions apply:

> ➤ If W answers about previous convictions: s 6 Criminal Procedure Act 1865
> ➤ If a party accuses W of bias
> ➤ If W has a reputation for untruthfulness
> ➤ If W has a disability that affects W's reliability

Hostile and unfavourable Ws

The general rule is that a party cannot attack the credibility of their own W. However, if the judge decides, on application by a party or of her own motion that a W is **not willing to tell the truth at the request of their own party** then W will be a 'hostile W'. Hostile Ws can be XX and their credibility attacked although it is clearly not a desirable method of examination.

Use of previous consistent statements

Previous consistent statements may not be relied upon as evidence of consistency, except:

- ➤ With the court's permission
- ➤ To rebut an allegation of recent fabrication
- ➤ To memory-refresh a W, with the court's permission

Use of previous inconsistent statements

While a W cannot rely upon their previous consistent statement, a party may wish to XX a W on a previous inconsistent statement.

If W accepts making the statement it will be admissible. If W does not accept making the statement, the party can prove the statement. W must be asked before the statement is proved.

W may be XX on the statement without being shown the previous statement. However, in order to contradict W, W must be shown the previous statement.

27.7. Opinion evidence

The general rule is that Ws who are not qualified may only give evidence as to facts. Ws may not give opinions. The reason is that inferences to be drawn from facts are a matter for the judge.

A common exception is where describing the underlying facts would be excessively onerous. For example, W may describe somebody as 'about 40 years old' (an opinion), when stating all the underlying facts (their hair colour, build, demeanour, dress) would be too onerous.

27.8. Character evidence

Character evidence can be relevant in three situations and its use depends on the situation.

Character is the fact in issue
Firstly, character can be the fact in issue (e.g. a defamation claim). Evidence as to character is admissible.

Character relevant to a fact in issue
Secondly, character can be relevant to a fact in issue (e.g. showing W has copied in other cases as evidence of W's copying in the present case).

In such a case the good character of W cannot be adduced. The bad character of W is admissible so long as it:
  ➢ Is logically probative
  ➢ It is not unfair
  ➢ The opposition has fair notice

Character relevant to credibility
Thirdly, character can be relevant to credibility (e.g. showing W is a habitual liar).

In such a case good character cannot be adduced simply to bolster credibility. However, if W's character has been attacked, W may defend himself.

Bad character can be used to discredit W so long as it is relevant. The judge has a duty to prevent questioning that is improper or oppressive.

Previous convictions: s 11 Civil Evidence Act 1968
Evidence of a previous subsiting conviction may be used in civil proceedings where it is relevant to any issue. A person will be presumed to have committed the offence unless it is proved otherwise.

Any evidence of the conviction will be admissible and certified documents are presumed true.

EXPERT EVIDENCE

27.9. Definition of an expert

An expert ('E') is a person who:
> Has relevant expertise
> Is aware of the overriding duty to the court and is able to fulfil it

27.10. Form of expert reports: PD 35

Expert reports must be written and addressed to the court. They must:
> Contain a statement of E's qualifications
> Outline who has carried out any examinations and whether they were carried out under E's supervision
> State any qualifications to E's opinion
> Summarize conclusions reached

Where there is a range of opinions that range must be summarized and reasons for E's opinion must be given.

An expert report must be verified by:
> A statement of truth
> A statement that E understands the duty to the court and has complied with it
> A statement that E understands CPR 35 and PD 35 and the Protocol for Instruction of Experts

27.11. Disclosure of reports and literature

Expert reports must be disclosed. If they are not disclosed they may not be relied upon.[122] Any disclosed may be relied upon as evidence.

Extent of disclosure
E must disclose:
> E's instructions[123]

---

[122] CPR 35.13

> What literature E has relied upon
> Any material not reasonably available to the opposing party[124]

Written questions to E: CPR 35.6

Parties may ask written questions of opposing Es. Questions must be asked no later than 28 days after disclosure of the report. E's answers form part of the report. If E does not answer, then a party may be prevented from relying upon E's report or face a costs sanction.

This process reduces the need for E to attend trial.

27.12. Use of secondary facts in expert reports

Secondary facts are the conclusions or inferences drawn from primary facts. The expert report must contain a statement of the primary facts relevant to E's (secondary) opinions. E must state which facts are in her knowledge and which are not.

27.13. Ultimate issues

Ultimate issues are issues that decide a case. Historically there was a prohibition on E giving evidence on ultimate issues but courts are now more flexible. It will be for the judge to decide whether or not to accept E's opinion.

27.14. Permission to use and call experts

Permission is required to call E or rely upon an expert report.[125] A party wishing to use expert evidence must provide:
> An estimate of E's costs
> The field in which E evidence is required
> The issues that E will address
> Where practicable, the name of E

---

[123] Although LPP is abrogated for E's instructions, the court will not allow questions on the instructions unless it is clear E's instructions were inadequate
[124] CPR 35.9
[125] CPR 35.4

Court's discretion over E evidence

The court may
- Direct a joint E:[126] (the normal rule in the fast track)
- Limit E's fees

---

[126] CPR 35.7

LEGAL PROFESSIONAL PRIVILEGE

Legal Professional Privilege ('LPP') is a status attaching to communications received from lawyers, and in some cases, TPs. LPP protects documents from inspection (see Chapter 15). The rationale is to encourage parties to be honest with their lawyers without the fear that their communication will be used in litigation.

27.15. Legal Advice Privilege

Litigation advice privilege covers all legal advice, assistance and 'wise counsel' **communicated** between a **client** and their **lawyer**. The lawyer must be a qualified lawyer: communications with a specialist tax accountant giving legal advice will not be covered by legal advice privilege.[127]

27.16. Litigation Privilege

Litigation privilege is both narrower and wider than legal advice privilege.

It is narrower in that it only applies to communications made with the **dominant purpose** of:
 ➤ Being used in litigation, or
 ➤ Obtaining advice about litigation

The litigation must be current or anticipated.

Litigation privilege is wider in that it protects not merely communications between a party and their lawyer, but **also between a party and a TP.**

---

[127] *R (on the application of Prudential plc & anr) v Special Commissioner of Income Tax & anr* [2013] UKSC 1

27.17. Crime / fraud limitation

LPP does not cover communications that are part of a crime or fraud, or which seek to legal advice to facilitate a fraud. Controversially, this limitation has been held to cover 'sharp' practice' that was not unlawful.[128]

27.18. Privilege against self-incrimination: s 14 Civil Evidence Act 1968

A party or W may refuse to answer questions or allow documents to be inspected if it might incriminate a party or W. There must be a **'real or appreciable' danger of prosecution.**

The court must decide if such a danger exists, but doubt will be resolved in favour of the party or W. The objection must be taken personally by W on oath.

27.19. Without prejudice communications

Communications that are **made with the purpose of settlement** of litigation are protected by without prejudice 'privilege'. Documents may be marked 'without prejudice' but the court will ignore the label (or lack of label) and look at the substance of the document.

Without prejudice communications that lead to settlement are admissible for the purpose of proving the settlement, and communications 'without prejudice save as to costs' are admissible for the purposes of assessing costs.

The protection attaches from the production of the document and applies in all proceedings. Wrongly using a without prejudice document at trial may lead to an aborted trial and wasted costs order.

---

[128] *Barclays Bank v Eustice* [1995] 4 All ER 511

27.20. Waiver of privilege

The protection given by privilege can be waived. Legal advice privilege and litigation privilege belong to the client and can only be waived by the client. The privilege against self-incrimination can only be waived by the party or W who would claim it. Without prejudice protection belongs to both parties and must be jointly waived.

27.21. Public Interest Immunity ('PII')

PII allows a party to withhold evidence on the ground that its inspection would prejudice the public interest. It must be **necessary** to withhold the evidence.

The procedure for a PII application is as follows:
> Party makes a without notice application
> The order must not be disclosed
> The court will rule on the application

PII has largely been replaced in civil proceedings by the Closed Material Procedure ('CMP'): <u>Part II, s 6 Justice and Security Act 2013.</u>

CHAPTER SUMMARY
> C bears the burden of proof on the balance of probabilities.
> There are three different types of hearsay with different procedural rules. Hearsay is always admissible.
> A W/S stands as a W's XIC.
> Permission must be sought to use expert evidence. A court may restrict expert evidence in different ways.
> LPP protects documents from inspection. It does not protect documents that are part of, or facilitate, a crime or fraud.

9539040R00088

Printed in Great Britain
by Amazon.co.uk, Ltd.,
Marston Gate.